Jean-Paul Sartre

Titles in the series Critical Lives present the work of leading cultural figures of the modern period. Each book explores the life of the artist, writer, philosopher or architect in question and relates it to their major works.

In the same series

Michel Foucault
David Macey

Jean Genet
Stephen Barber

Pablo Picasso
Mary Ann Caws

Franz Kafka
Sander L. Gilman

Guy Debord
Andy Merrifield

Marcel Duchamp
Caroline Cros

Frank Lloyd Wright
Robert McCarter

James Joyce
Andrew Gibson

Jean-Paul Sartre

Andrew Leak

REAKTION BOOKS

Published by Reaktion Books Ltd
33 Great Sutton Street
London EC1V ODX, UK

www.reaktionbooks.co.uk

First published 2006

Printed and bound in Great Britain
by CPI/Bath Press, Bath

British Library Cataloguing in Publication Data
Leak, Andrew N., 1956–
   Jean-Paul Sartre. – (Critical lives)
   1. Sartre, Jean Paul, 1905–1980 2. Philosophers – France – Biography
   I.Title
   194

ISBN 1 86189 270 5

Contents

Jean-Paul Sartre in 1946.

Preface

Following the appearance of the first three volumes of his biographical study of Flaubert, Sartre remarked that, had he been able
to spend just fifteen minutes in the company of the great novelist,
he would have been able to learn more about him than by reading
his entire voluminous correspondence. (Of course, this assumes
that Sartre would have been capable of remaining fifteen minutes
in Flaubert's company, as he was also convinced that Flaubert was
a crushing bore!) Like Freud, or like the Buddhists who were capable
of finding the whole world in a bean, Sartre fancied that the whole
of a subject's personality was present – at age fifteen or fifty – in his
every gesture or glance; existentially, if not ethically, drinking tea
rather than coffee, scratching one's ear with the index finger
rather than the auricular, preferring sauerkraut to oysters are as
significant as stealing from one's parents, talking under torture,
abandoning a pregnant partner, or devoting one's life to writing . . .
Of course, no biographer or critic will ever again be able spend
fifteen minutes in Sartre's presence, and, as Sartre himself might
have said, 'tant mieux'!

   When I first embarked on serious study of Sartre, friends and
mentors suggested that I might take myself off to Paris to meet
him. I have to confess that I felt a certain relief when, six months
later, Sartre died. Relief at no longer having to explain, to myself
or to others, why I felt no desire or curiosity to meet him: the
definitive two metres of texts on my bookshelf surely contained

more of 'Sartre' than I might hope to find in a blind old man dying in a Montparnasse apartment. Twenty-five years on, the two metres have become two-and-a-half, as 'Sartre' has continued to expand and mutate with each posthumous publication. Not only that: with each notable anniversary – and none could be more notable than the recent centenary of his birth – witnesses to his life, both real and purported, partisans and detractors, critics and exegetes, have rolled up to provide the illustrious zombie with ever more textual prosthetics. Sartre long since left Kafka and Borges, Joyce and Proust in his wake as the most written-about twentieth-century author. But why? His works do not possess the spectacular verbal richness of Joyce or Proust, nor do they tease their readers, like those of Kafka or Borges, with the promise of a meaning always on the point of disclosure. The question as to why Sartre and his work have stimulated so many readers to read, so many writers to write, so many thinkers to think and so many critics to critique is one that is surely worth considering. Had Sartre worked all his life as a librarian in Buenos Aires or toiled as an obscure clerk in a Mitteleuropa insurance agency, I doubt his works would have attracted the readership they did; which is to say that his work, more than any other, has become inseparable from the image of the man himself.

This book does not propose a radical re-evaluation of the Sartrean corpus: the readings are my own, but I am not the only one to have read in this way. My aim is to sketch the ways in which a life may become 'written' – by the one who is living it, by those who share it and by those who come after; to explore what is at stake in such a 'writing'; and, finally, to suggest why it may still be worth reading today.

1

A Child in the Hall of Mirrors

One appears to begin at the beginning ... but the end is already there and it transforms everything. For us, the guy is already the hero of the story.

La Nausée

On 17 September 1906 a certain Jean-Baptiste Sartre lay dying in a small farm near Thiviers in southwest France. As the enterocolitis he had contracted seven years earlier in China closed down his body, he would doubtless have been perplexed to learn that 80 years hence an assiduous scholar would visit his birthplace, scrutinize records of his naval career, and read letters he had written home from his overseas postings in an attempt to find out what kind of man he had been. What had he done to deserve such attention? Nothing but his duty – his duty as a husband, that is: one day in the autumn of 1904 he had inseminated Anne-Marie Sartre, née Schweitzer, whom he had married the previous May. The issue of this 'immense stupidity' was at that moment in September 1906 giving vent to his resentment in the home of the wet nurse where he had been placed in order to allow his mother to devote her energies to nursing her dying husband. The baby, born on 21 June 1905 and baptized Jean-Paul-Charles-Aymard Sartre, would one day become 'Sartre', thus rescuing his father from oblivion and endowing him with a kind of vicarious immortality: the son gives birth to the father. But when, half a century later, Sartre came to put his own life into words, his father merited no more than a few lines: 'Even today, I am amazed at how little I know about him. And yet, he loved, he tried to live, he found himself dying; that is enough to make a whole man.'[1] We should not be misled by the terseness of this obituary: to learn to be a 'whole man' is no little thing in Sartre's view of humanity.

The death of Jean-Baptiste left Anne-Marie virtually without financial support and without a roof over her head, so she went back to live with her parents in Meudon. Her father, Charles Schweitzer, had taken early retirement from teaching, but with extra mouths to feed, he rescinded his notice. There was not a word of complaint, everyone behaved impeccably, but the reproaches were no less real for not being articulated: 'families, of course, prefer widows to young single mothers, but only just'.[2] In the bourgeois worldview that sees marriage as more of a business partnership than an expression of love, Anne-Marie had clearly been fobbed off with damaged goods. Sartre himself later saw the loss of his father as the determining moment of his life: condemning his mother to ten years of filial servitude, it liberated the child, in advance, from a father–son relationship that would inevitably, he imagined, have crushed him: 'The death of Jean-Baptiste . . . returned my mother to her chains and gave me my freedom.'[3]

And so began ten years of 'happiness' for 'Poulou'.

Les Mots (the autobiography that Sartre wrote in his fifties) lays no claim to objective truthfulness. Indeed, after 50 pages, we are disconcerted to read: 'What I have just written is false. True. Neither true nor false, like everything one writes about madmen, about men.'[4] In later years Sartre took to referring to the biographies he wrote as 'true novels', adding that he would like *Les Mots*, too, to be read as a novel, albeit 'one in which [I] believe'. Bearing in mind these caveats surrounding the veracity of the account, let us now sketch the outline of the story that Sartre tells about his own childhood in *Les Mots*.

All artists are victims of a fundamental ambiguity: with one foot in the imaginary and one in the real, they are – to use an image beloved of Sartre – like mermaids whose human form finishes in a fish's tail. In short, they are monsters. *Les Mots* is marked by this tension between the real and the imaginary, and is Sartre's attempt to account for the choices that led him to become such a monster. Poulou – as the child Sartre was known in his family – appears in the Schweitzer household as the result of an almost immaculate conception: Anne-Marie is, after all, 'a virgin with a stain'. Deprived of a father, he is also deprived of a destiny. A father would at least have given him something to revolt against. But, burdensome as it may be, the Father's law at least keeps the son anchored in reality. The absence of a father had endowed him with an 'incredible lightness' that, at times, became unbearable.

As ill luck would have it, the environment in which he was to spend his early childhood was less likely than most to provide him with solid roots in reality. Throughout *Les Mots* Sartre employs the pun available in French on the adjective *vrai*: both 'true' and 'real'. The Schweitzers enact, on a daily basis, the *comédie familiale*, presided over by the arch buffoon himself, Charles. In this comedy of manners, nothing is ever quite true (true feelings are translated into the rituals of bourgeois politeness) and nothing is ever quite real. Poulou discovers that he has been given the leading role: he is to play the bundle of joy, and later the child prodigy who will enable Charles to perfect the 'Art of Being a Grandfather'; Louise and Anne-Marie have walk-on parts: Louise is the cynical, some-what grumpy grandmother who is not taken in by Poulou's play-acting; Anne-Marie has few lines: ever the dutiful daughter.

In short, Poulou became an imaginary child locked in an im-aginary world. Worse, he became an 'appalling little child-king',[5] ministered to by an entourage of simpering courtiers. The company of his peers could have 'saved' him, but he was educated at home until the age of ten by his grandfather and his mother.

Paradoxically, the disease turned out to be the cure: 'everything took place in my head; an imaginary child, I defended myself by imagination'.[6] Soon he would 'defend himself' with a pen in his hand, but before writing came reading. Having, apparently, taught himself to read, Poulou proceeded to devour the contents of his grandfather's library. The latter contained everything one might expect to find in the library of a nineteenth-century citizen of the Republic of Letters, and so it was that the child became imbued with the culture and ideology that had held sway a half-century before, during the Second Empire. Whether Poulou actually enjoyed reading Rabelais, Corneille, Racine, Voltaire and Vigny is uncertain, but it is clear that he could have understood very little of them: how does a seven-year-old grasp the notion of honour in Corneille? And just what were Emma Bovary and Léon *doing* in the back of that carriage as it careered through the streets of Rouen? Constantly under the gaze of the adults, mimicking the posture of the reader-engrossed-in-his-book, Poulou was as much a phoney reader as he was a phoney child. Fortunately for him, his mother and grandmother were less enthusiastic than Charles at the prospect of his metamorphosis into a bookworm before their very eyes. The remedy was simply to provide him with reading more suited to his age and understanding. This initially took the form of popular comic books and, very soon, the children's classics: Jules Verne, *Nicholas Nickelby*, *The Last of the Mohicans*. Sartre refers to these as 'de *vraies* lectures' ('*real* books'). It is interesting that, in the so-potent opposition between real and imaginary, the 'real' or the 'true' is associated with the *minor*: minor literature (comics, children's books, detective fiction), cinema (as an art form in its infancy) and minors themselves: the children whose games in the Jardins du Luxembourg he could only witness from the lonely sidelines.

While these books may have put him back in touch with the truth of his childhood, they did so by deploying 'falsehood': the real can only be approached through the imaginary. Long before he discovered philosophical idealism, Poulou was – like all children – a thoroughgoing idealist: encountering the world first in the pages of the *Grand Larousse* encyclopædia, he fell victim to a fallacy that he would take 30 years to grow out of:

It was in books that I first encountered the world: assimilated, classified, labeled, filtered through thought, but still redoubtable; and I confused the disorder of my reading experiences with the random course of events in the world. That is the origin of the idealism that it has taken me thirty years to get rid of.[7]

Carried over from reading into writing, this idealism had decisive consequences.

His first 'novel' was called 'For a Butterfly' and it was plagiarized in its entirety from a comic book he had read. The idealist illusion is intact: 'Each thing humbly asked to be named, and to do so was, in the same movement, to create it and to appropriate it. Without this capital illusion, I would never have become a writer.'[8] The invention of writing by the child was his means of self-invention: the child-monster, contorted and twisted out of shape by the mutilating gaze of the adults, could now start to become simply a child: 'I was born of writing; before writing there was just a play of reflections; I knew, when I wrote my first novel, that a child had slipped into the hall of mirrors.'[9] Everything hinges on the passage from one pronoun to another: from 'I' to 'He'. It matters little that the 'He' is the simple embodiment of the desires, fears and fantasies of the 'I', what counts is that they are *formally* distinct. This translation affords the writer the secret pleasure of indulging and disavowing his desires at one and the same time: 'I experienced the thrill of being *him*, without his being entirely me.'[10]

However, this enabling discovery was accompanied by an additional imposture. Dismayed at the prospect of his grandson becoming a professional writer – a class of person for whom he had the utmost contempt – Charles diverted Poulou's ambitions towards an altogether nobler goal: he would become – like generations of Schweitzers – a teacher; a teacher who would, incidentally, also write. Charles foresaw a destiny of quiet mediocrity for Poulou; the child transformed it into a dream of literary immortality. He would exercise the thankless profession of teacher in some small provincial town, but would all the while be filling notebook after notebook with unread and unrecognized masterpieces. The fantasy varied, but one version went like this: upon his death, some former students would take it upon themselves to sort out and edit his notes; amongst these notes they would discover the Lost Masterpiece, the work that would save humanity. Other versions saw fame arrive in the lifetime of the author, but always too late: recognition coincided with death:

> One thing strikes me in this tale repeated a thousand times: the day that I see my name in the paper, something snaps inside me, I am finished . . . The two *dénouements* amount to the same thing: whether I die to be reborn into glory, or glory comes first and kills me, the desire to write conceals a refusal to live.[11]

What Sartre refers to as his 'neurosis' in *Les Mots* was, essentially, the belief in the possibility of salvation through art. On the one hand, this was a salvation of each moment: the physical practice of writing – conducted daily throughout his life with the meticulousness of a monk going about his spiritual exercises – provided an instant 'fix' of salvation: the limp, formless, meaningless flow of existence was replaced by a world that had a beginning, a middle and an end. What is more, the end reflected its necessity back onto the beginning and the middle. The imaginary child becomes real by proxy: 'Depicting real objects with real words traced with a real pen, it would be pretty damn surprising if I didn't become real too.'[12] Additionally, the neurosis was a veritable eschatology. From the age of nine – if we are to believe *Les Mots* – Sartre was convinced that he was *already* a great writer. Great writers produce great works but they need a lifetime to do so; death cannot come before the work is complete: as long as the work is 'in progress' the writer cannot die. Thus the *œuvre* becomes a talisman, and the daily practice of writing – as in the story of Scheherezade – becomes a matter of life and death.

In October 1915 Sartre entered the Lycée Henri-IV. In the two years he spent there his 'neurosis' seems to have entered a kind of 'latency period': 'as for that mandate that had been deposited inside me in a sealed envelope by the adults, I no longer thought about it, but it was still there.'[13]

The narrative of *Les Mots* effectively ends in 1917, when Sartre was in *cinquième* (the equivalent of Year 7 in the UK). The reason for this was that 1917 marked a veritable rupture in his life. On 28 April of that year, Anne-Marie married Joseph Mancy, a graduate – like her brother Georges – of the prestigious science and engineering school, the Ecole Polytechnique. The marriage solved all of Anne-Marie's problems at a stroke: she was acquiring financial security, social standing, an end to the prolonged dependency on her parents, an ally in the interminable and unseemly wrangles over property inheritance in Thiviers that had been the bane of her existence since her first husband's death, and a father for her soon-to-be teenage son. It is certain, however, that Poulou did not view this new situation quite so positively. How could he? As for Mancy, he could have combined the wisdom of Solomon and the patience of Job, and the boy would still have loathed him, seeing him as the usurper come to contest his 'untroubled possession'[14] of his mother. In any case, what little is known of Mancy suggests that he did not possess these biblical qualities in abundance. The son of a Lyon railway worker, Mancy had, in 1917, risen to become the director of the Delaunay-Belleville shipyards in La Rochelle, where in 1920 he would distinguish himself as a strike-breaker. Such was his bourgeois conventionality that he refused to the end of his life even to meet Sartre's companion, Simone de Beauvoir, on the grounds that she and Sartre were neither married nor engaged! Worse, he was a 'scientist'. Out went the liberal arts and in came the exact sciences. We will never know how Mancy himself viewed his responsibilities towards his stepson, nor how he actually acquitted himself of these, but it is certain that the moment he stepped into that role he was destined to join Commander Aupick in the ranks of literature's most-hated stepfathers.[15] What was evidently a cultural dislocation for the child was accompanied by a no less significant physical relocation: at the end of the school year of 1917, the new family unit moved to La Rochelle.

On the rare occasions that Sartre could be persuaded to recall his adolescence, the themes that recur are violence and humiliation. The violence was probably little more than the banal violence of adolescent boys, but it is likely that the routine cruelty of adolescence was exacerbated by the fact that France was at war. Although La Rochelle was far removed from the front, the war was ever-present: supply ships were torpedoed off the coast, and the town's station was constantly awash with reinforcements on their way to the front and with prisoners-of-war returning from it. More importantly, the men were away at the war, leaving the boys with the impression that they had suddenly become the man of the household. Sartre's retrospective interpretation of this violence saw in it a form of class warfare specific to the social demographics of La Rochelle. He was at the boys' grammar school of La Rochelle. This school found itself caught between the decidedly aristocratic pupils of the Collège Fénelon and the 'yobs' who had already left school in order to embrace a trade. The streets of La Rochelle were the scene of frequent running battles between these factions. As if the daily violence outside the school were not enough, the young Sartre had to suffer the bullying and the taunts of his classmates. With his Parisian accent, his precious speech habits, his antiquated literary culture – not to mention his plus fours and his outrageous squint – Sartre presented eccentricities aplenty. He became, by his account at least, the whipping-boy of the school, but fought back with all the force that his diminutive stature afforded him. In order to curry favour with his tormentors, he once again defended himself with his imagination, inventing fictional girlfriends. His confabulations were discovered for what they were and simply added to the scorn poured on his head. If the prestige of an unlikely sexual prowess eluded him, perhaps he could purchase the good will of his peers? He took to stealing small change from his mother in order to offer sweets and cakes to his 'friends'. When the thefts were discovered, his misery was compounded. The torture of La Rochelle came to an end when Sartre fell ill in the summer of 1920 and was repatriated to Paris.

He re-entered Henri-iv as a day-boarder and was reunited with his friend Paul Nizan whom he had met there three years earlier. Having taken the *baccalauréat* in 1922, he decided, with Nizan, to move to the Lycée Louis-le-Grand in order to prepare the entrance examination for the Ecole Normale Supérieure (ENS). The ENS was, at the time, the most prestigious of the so-called *Grandes Ecoles* which formed the Republic's political elites. Two years of intensive preparation – *hypokhâgne* and *khâgne* – were required in order to take the highly competitive entrance examination. The years 1922–24 saw the appearance of Sartre's first published fiction. His 'vocation' was spurred by competition with the more precociously talented Nizan, as evidenced by the relationship between their fictional counterparts in *La Semence et le Scaphandre*.[16] This tale revolves around the birth of a literary review, and it was just such a student-run review – bearing the vaguely Surrealist title *La Revue sans Titre* – that published Sartre's *L'Ange du morbide* and several chapters of *Jésus la Chouette*. The style of these early pieces is stilted and frequently sententious. Yet there are elements here that a reader of the mature Sartre would immediately recognize as 'Sartrean': the portrayal of morbid sexuality (in *L'Ange du morbide*); or, more generally, the fierce satire of bourgeois respectability and the practice of narrative irony. The narrator of *La Semence et le Scaphandre* remarks at one point:

> Finally, I made a short novel out of an adventure that had befallen me some little time before; it earned me a certain success amongst a narrow circle of readers and this modest triumph prompted in me the resolution no longer to write anything that was not founded in the events of my own life.[17]

The use of a first-person narrator and the heavy reliance on auto-biographical elements are common enough in juvenilia, but this quotation raises a question that is of central concern to us: what is the relation that binds the works of a writer to the life in which those works are inscribed as events? There are other recognizably Sartrean traits in these very early texts that are worthy of mention. Betrayal, for example. The narrators of *Jésus la Chouette* and *La Semence et le Scaphandre* undoubtedly embody important aspects of Sartre's own self, but they are distanced (through irony), disavowed and, finally, betrayed by their creator in a characteristic movement of *dissociation*. These literary creatures are, to use the language of psychoanalysis, simultaneously 'me' and 'not-me' objects.[18]

When Sartre entered *prépa* in 1922, what exactly was he preparing himself for? Death or Glory! In Sartre's personal mythology, death was the sad mediocrity of the provincial teacher who was also a 'Sunday writer': the destiny foretold by his grandfather. Since the ENS led most surely into a teaching career of some description, to choose that path was clearly to flirt with death itself. Glory was a far less certain outcome than a secure teaching job in a *lycée* or a university.

It was not until his second year at Louis-le-Grand that Sartre discovered the joys of philosophy, having previously regarded it as a rather dry discipline. It was thus as a philosophy student that

The 18-year-old Jean-Paul Sartre.

Sartre entered the ENS in 1924. In so doing, he was joining a veritable intellectual elite. The style of philosophy that held sway at the ENS at that time was the critical, or rationalist, idealism practised by its leading philosopher, Léon Brunschvicg. For his part, Sartre apparently harboured at that point no ambition to become an *original* philosopher. In at least two respects, he regarded philosophy as a mere adjunct to the real activity of his life – writing. First, he would have to support himself while writing, and teaching philosophy was one way of earning a living. Second, he saw philosophical investigation as complementing the activity of the writer: the writer's job was to *unveil truths* about the world and about the human condition, and where better to discover these truths than in philosophy? But the dominant mode of continental philosophy did not quite fit the bill: 'I was a realist at the time, out of a taste for feeling the resistance of things . . . I couldn't enjoy a landscape or a sky unless I thought it *was* exactly as I *saw* it.'[19] His realism was also, characteristically, a reaction against himself – against the chronic idealism of the writer who privileges the word over the object. It was only when he discovered phenomenology, several years later, that he was able to effect some kind of resolution of these warring idealist and realist tendencies.

Sartre described the years he spent at ENS as the happiest of his life, and it is not hard to appreciate why. It was at *Normale Sup'* that he started fashioning for himself an enduring persona in the eyes of others: he was the voracious reader, the tireless writer with a seemingly infinite capacity for hard work; but he was also the multi-talented variety artist: singing (he had a fine voice), acting, performing impressions of his peers and his professors, playing the piano, improvising sketches, organizing rags. In short, he turned himself into the court-jester, but woe betide anyone who got on the wrong side of him: he had a fearsome reputation for sarcasm, wit and verbal violence. He made himself into the very opposite of the too-delicate, too-cosseted little boy who had shivered on the sidelines as the other boys went about their rough-and-tumble in the Luxembourg Gardens.

In 1925, at the funeral of his young cousin Annie in Thiviers, Sartre met Simone Jollivet and commenced his first serious love affair – conducted, albeit, at long distance: Simone lived in Toulouse. The affair was tempestuous and hit the rocks many times before petering out into 'mere' friendship. But the surviving letters that Sartre wrote to her in 1926–28 reveal a great deal about his intellectual and sentimental development. A letter of 1926 contains the earliest known autobiographical sketch. In this letter, he comments on the construction of his persona: 'I took an early dislike to myself and the first thing that I really constructed was my own character.'[20] But the creation of a 'character' or 'persona' implies a certain relation to other people. They are needed insofar as they serve as mirrors in which the 'I' can contemplate the 'me' he has created. Sartre's advice to Simone on relations with other people has a distinctly 'Nietzschean' ring about it: 'Obviously, you have to live with others, but you must never allow them to gain . . . so much influence over you, or become so indispensable to you that you can't just tell them to go to hell when you feel like it.'[21] His ideas on what it is to be free were even more Nietzschean: 'If . . . you develop in yourself the strength and the violence of the passions, whilst suppressing all scruples and all pity, then you will be absolutely free.'[22] No surprise to learn, then, that Sartre and Nizan thought of themselves as 'supermen', condemned to live apart from the common herd by virtue of their superior intellect and their ascetic morality. Already, Sartre saw himself as the man who sets out to think outside of and against existing authority and existing systems of morality; the man who contests even himself; the self-creation, the creature of his own works; the outsider . . . It was for Simone Jollivet that Sartre wrote a novel entitled *Une Défaite*, based very closely on the famous triangle of Nietzsche, Wagner and Cosima. The novel remained, thankfully, unpublished.

Sartre's four years at the ENS should have culminated in 1928 with the written paper of the *agrégation de philosophie*. To general astonishment, he failed: he had tried to be too original in his treatment of the given subject and had been penalized for it. Not that he seems to have taken it too badly. Indeed, failure, in this instance, may well have saved him from a life of bourgeois mediocrity: he had, some little time before, become 'vaguely engaged' to the sister of one of his friends; clearly deciding that the young man had no future, her parents promptly called off the engagement. When he retook the examination in 1929 he was placed first. The written subject was 'Contingency and Freedom'. The term 'contingent' belongs to the technical vocabulary of philosophy, and denotes the opposite of 'necessary': a contingent event is one that may or may not occur; a contingent thing is one that may or may not be. It remains thereafter at the centre of all of his reflections, unassailable, like a mathematical or logical axiom. The philosopher Raymond Aron – who had been Sartre's friend at ENS – recalled that he first heard Sartre develop his personal ideas on contingency in a paper that he gave in one of Brunschvicg's seminars in 1927–28. But the *intuition* of contingency had more distant origins. Sartre asserts in *Les Mots* that he had such an intuition from a very early age. Deprived of a 'mandate to exist', the child experienced himself as one of nature's random events: writing was what he had invented in order to justify the fact of his being there.

At some point in the academic year 1928–29 – accounts vary as to exactly when – Sartre began a relationship that would shape the rest of his life. He had noticed a young woman in the year below (the year he now rejoined, of course) whom he had declared to be 'nice, pretty, but terribly dressed'. She, for her part, had long been aware of the ringleader of a prestigious group of students in the year above, reputed to be brilliant but 'dangerous': there were dark rumours of excessive drinking, turbulent behaviour, and even womanizing. The young woman, Simone de Beauvoir, was from a Catholic bourgeois family but was in the process of kicking over the traces of a stultifyingly conventional and sheltered education. She saw in Sartre just the man to help her do precisely that. It is impossible, here, to do justice to the importance of this relationship for both parties: for the next 51 years they were constant companions. The strength of the relationship seems to have derived from a powerful intellectual and affective complementarity. Each had found the *double* s/he had been seeking (one of Sartre's favourite terms of endearment for his companion was 'you other myself'). Once they had found each other, all other friendships became secondary. The term 'double' should also be taken here with its full psychoanalytic charge: in their voluminous published correspondence, it is striking how much Sartre masculinizes Beauvoir and feminizes himself. She is his 'judge', his 'stern censor', his 'paragon'. Gleefully confessing his misdeeds, he appears to wish to draw down upon himself the full severity of her judgement: he is the child and she the mother. At other times the roles are reversed and she becomes her father's little girl. Presumably the strength of the bond lay in the reversibility of the roles. Mutual infantilization, of course, is part of any love relationship – a glance at the personal columns on Valentine's Day is enough to confirm this – but one senses a profound catharsis here: the 'masculinity' of Beauvoir allowed Sartre to acknowledge a feminine side to himself, which had been firmly suppressed in the aggressively male atmosphere of *khâgne* and ENS. Only occasionally had it been discernible: for example, in the 'indefinable tenderness' of the relationship between Sartre and Nizan as it is dramatized in *La Semence et le Scaphandre*.

No sooner had the relationship begun that it was interrupted. In autumn 1929 Sartre left to do his military service. At St-Cyr, he was initiated into the mysteries of meteorology. Before the separation he had laid down some ground-rules, proposing a two-year 'lease': travel, transparency (complete mutual honesty) and polygamy! In fact, this was an ingenious rationalization, deploying the notion of contingency to good effect: he explained to her that they could each have 'contingent' love affairs, but that the only 'necessary' one was theirs. Initially at least, Sartre made freer use of this arrangement than did Beauvoir.

Still horrified at the prospect of becoming a provincial teacher, Sartre had applied for a post as *lecteur* in Japan, to commence on his release from the army. It was therefore with dismay that he learned in 1931 that, rather than Japan, he was to be sent to teach at the *lycée* in Le Havre. To make matters worse, Beauvoir was appointed in Marseille, at the other end of France.

For a man who considered ambition to be his deepest character trait, and who planned his life like a novel with a happy ending, the posting to Le Havre represented a severe setback. His literary ambitions, in particular, had taken a knock when *Une défaite* and

La Légende de la vérité were rejected by publishers. Perhaps he had been mistaken about his genius? Perhaps he was destined to end his days, like 'Jésus la Chouette', as a reviled teacher in some provincial backwater? His reaction was characteristic: to go back to his books, to work harder, to read more and to write more. This is a pattern that was repeated throughout his life: every time he made an expansive movement towards the world, towards other people, that was rebuffed, his first movement was to retreat back into himself to repair his wounded narcissism, back into the imaginary or into the pure exercise of the intellect – into a place where it was always safe and warm. But this is not to imply that he lived like a hermit in Le Havre. On the contrary, one tactic he had evolved to protect himself was, paradoxically, to *vivre public* (to live publicly). This involved the construction of a public persona that he could then joyfully abandon to other people. This persona was not necessarily false or at odds with some mysterious, incommunicable inner self, but the very fact that it had been disowned served to differentiate it from the 'I' that had disowned it, thus setting in motion an endless cycle of 'dissociation'. Sartre would later describe this way of being with other people as 'a total lack of solidarity with myself'.[23]

At the Lycée François 1ᵉʳ where he taught, he was, by all accounts, unconventional, informal, inspirational and occasionally daunting. As early as this, he instinctively championed the individual over the system – giving pass marks to students whom other teachers would have failed without compunction, and challenging his students to *think for themselves*. There may seem nothing exceptional in this, but one must remember that for most of the twentieth century the French education system did little to foster or encourage original thought. From this time, he started to collect 'disciples' amongst his students: most of those who would join his closest circle of friends – the so-called 'family' – were his or Beauvoir's former students. The first of these 'disciples' was a young man named Jacques-Laurent

Bost, who was the younger brother of the novelist and screenwriter Pierre Bost. 'Little Bost' would later be immortalized in the character of Boris in Sartre's novel trilogy, *Les Chemins de la liberté*. Despite his near despair at being in Le Havre in the first place, he threw himself enthusiastically into the intellectual life of the *lycée* and the city, giving a memorable speech on the cinema at the 1931 prize-giving, and delivering a series of public lectures on topics ranging from German philosophy to the contemporary novel. His 'real' life was elsewhere, however. In a letter of October 1931 to Beauvoir, Sartre confides that he had been to

> that quarter of Le Havre that I like so much and that I've decided to put into my 'factum' on Contingency. It's true, everything really is contingent there, even the sky, which by any measure of meteorological likelihood should be the same over the whole of Le Havre: but it isn't.[24]

The 'factum' was the name Sartre gave to his new philosophico-literary project – a 'factum' being a polemical pamphlet. From the outset, the project was a hybrid: neither philosophical treatise nor novel, it would occupy Sartre for the next seven years, and pass through numerous mutations before emerging in 1938 as *La Nausée*. Le Havre appears in that novel, thinly disguised, as 'Bouville'; on Sartre's death, the town would repay that ambiguous homage: the street where the *lycée* is situated was renamed rue Jean-Paul Sartre.

Early in 1933 an encounter took place that was to prove as decisive for Sartre's philosophical orientation as it did for his literary development. One evening, he and Beauvoir met for a drink with their friend Raymond Aron – who was taking a sabbatical year at the French Institute in Berlin. Pointing to a glass, Aron said: 'You see, my little friend, if you are a phenomenologist, you can talk about this cocktail and its philosophy!'[25] Upon which, reportedly, Sartre paled with emotion! Phenomenology was a philosophical method developed by the German philosopher Edmund Husserl that involved bracketing-off, or setting aside all preconceptions and prior knowledge about the world in order to describe the phenomenon as it *appears* to consciousness. The *noumenal* essence of the object (what it is in itself) can only be discovered by means of this stage of pure description of the *phenomenon* (the way the object presents itself to consciousness). Sartre had long been hostile to introspection and self-indulgent subjectivism; he had also long been aware of his 'characterological' tendency to dissociate his present self from his past selves – even to the point where the very notion of a 'stable' self becomes problematic. In Husserl he found confirmation of 'this necessity for consciousness to exist as consciousness of something other than itself'.[26] A necessity that renders introspection futile. When we look 'inside' consciousness, we find only 'a flight from itself, a slipping outside of itself'.[27] This is what Husserl – borrowing from the Austrian philosopher Brentano – calls *intentionality*, and which can be summarized in the dictum 'All consciousness is consciousness *of* something'.

The meeting with Aron prompted Sartre to apply to succeed him in Berlin for the academic year 1933–34. That year was spent in the intensive study of Husserl (morning), writing the 'factum' (late afternoon), strolling in Berlin and pursuing various 'contingent' love affairs. Sartre's total immersion in Husserl, for the next six years, did not imply a master–student relationship: how could the consummate narcissist accept the tutelage of a master – even a *maître à penser*? Indeed, in 1937 he published a work – *La Transcendance de l'ego* – whose premise contradicts Husserl's view of the ego while radicalizing the latter's anti-subjectivism. In this work Sartre seeks to demonstrate that, far from being 'inside' consciousness, the ego is itself 'out there in the world', an object for consciousness, but transcendent of any single moment of consciousness: as (in)accessible to oneself as it is to others.

The return to Le Havre and the life of the provincial teacher was hard. Some things had changed for the better: Beauvoir was much closer – she now had a post in Rouen. Others had got worse: he recounts in *Les Carnets de la drôle de guerre* how he had looked in the mirror one day to notice that his hair was starting to thin. Moreover, he was approaching that symbolic age of 30, and fame still eluded him! In his notepad he had copied an aphorism to the effect that the man who is not famous by the age of 28 can forget about glory forever. Well, 28 had been and gone. The comparisons with his friend Nizan were all too obvious: by 1934 Nizan was already an established author with two novels under his belt; since 1927 he had also thrown himself into a life of political activism with the Parti Communiste Français (PCF). Things that stayed the same were perhaps even more depressing. The relationship with Beauvoir, for example, appeared to have settled into something resembling a routine.

But the stability of the couple was shaken by the irruption into their lives in 1934 of one of Beauvoir's formers pupils at Rouen, Olga Kosakiewicz, who was the daughter of a White Russian émigré and a French woman. The couple became a trio, a pattern that would recur throughout Sartre and Beauvoir's long relationship. Sartre conceived a passion for Olga that had all the force of a premature midlife crisis. The distorting filter of his infatuation, coupled with anxiety over the stagnation of his own existence, transformed what a more dispassionate observer might have seen as immaturity, insecurity and posturing on the part of the young woman into spontaneity, unpredictability and 'authenticity'. Beauvoir's fictionalized account of the trio in her first novel, *L'Invitée* (1943), suggests that she was more clear-sighted about the virtues of Olga, despite, or perhaps because of, her evident jealousy. It is clear from the long and detailed account that Beauvoir gives of the trio in her memoirs that Sartre's mood swung violently between besotted indulgence and jealous rage; he would drive Beauvoir to distraction by insisting on analysing, with her, the merest word that Olga had uttered, the subtlest inflection of tone, the slightest glance she had given him. This mode of mental functioning comes close to paranoia, and there is no doubt that Sartre's mental state at this period had not exactly been helped by another, quite unrelated incident. As part of the research for a book he was writing on the image, Sartre had had himself injected with mescaline – by a doctor friend – in order to explore the nature of hallucinations. The hallucinations lasted for far longer than is normal and took a decidedly nastier turn than Sartre had expected. Still worse, in spring 1936, *Melancholia* – as the 'factum' was now called – was rejected by Gallimard. It would be hard to overstate the impact of this blow. But things were about to take a turn for the better. The novel may have been rejected, but he was, finally, emerging into print: the book on the image, *L'Imagination*, was published in 1936 and *La Transcendance de l'ego* a year later. Then finally, in April 1937, thanks to the efforts of a former pupil, Jacques-Laurent Bost, and the husband of a former lover, the theatre director Charles Dullin, who had married Simone Jollivet, *Melancholia* was provisionally accepted for publication by Gallimard. Not only was the novel accepted, but Gallimard also agreed to publish in the prestigious *Nouvelle Revue Française* a number of Sartre's short stories, starting with 'Le Mur' in July 1937. Moreover, Sartre had transferred his passion for Olga onto her younger sister Wanda, who proved, eventually, to be more accommodating than her older sister had been when it came to the physical consummation of that passion. Finally, from 1937 both Sartre and Beauvoir were at last 'back home', having secured posts in Paris at the Lycée Pasteur and the Lycée Molière respectively. 'Little Bost' incidentally (is it really 'incidental'?) would later marry Olga Kosakiewicz, whilst secretly she remained Beauvoir's lover for a further fifteen years: from the outset, Sartre's 'family' had an incestuous cohesion.

Of all Sartre's works, his first novel undoubtedly owes the most to the hand of others, starting with the title. Brice Parain – the Gallimard editor assigned to the project – told Sartre that 'Melancholia' would not do. What about *Les Aventures extraordinaires d'Antoine Roquentin?*, responded Sartre. Finally, it was Gaston Gallimard himself who came up with the title that now seems so self-evident: *La Nausée*. The text itself was severely cut at Parain's insistence and on Beauvoir's advice; these cuts were designed to make the text sharper and less ponderous, but also to make it less scabrous: this was 1938 after all, and even the title was considered by some to be in bad taste. The novel that hit the book stalls in April 1938 was a much leaner and more focused text than the one submitted a year earlier. The novel is now recognized as a 'classic' of twentieth-century world literature, and its protagonist – Antoine Roquentin – has been identified, along with Camus's Meursault, as one of the iconic 'outsiders' of that century.

Despite the passing years, *La Nausée* has retained its ability to disorientate, and not only on first reading. The novel is presented as the diary of one Antoine Roquentin. It is unclear as to why we should be reading this diary: a note from 'The Editors' tells us that it was found among the papers of Roquentin, but we never know whether Roquentin is dead or alive, or what great deeds – laudable or ignominious – may have caused the 'Editors' to deem his diary worthy of publication. An internally consistent dating places the 'action' in one month: from Monday 25 January 1932 to Wednesday 24 February 1932. The diary entries chronicle the banal existence of their author. Having travelled extensively in the Far East, Roquentin has returned to live in Bouville in order to conduct historical research in the town library for a biography of an eighteenth-century aristocratic adventurer, M. de Rollebon. A man of independent means, Roquentin has little or no contact with the Bouvillois, beyond the occasional reluctant lunch with a self-taught man (the 'autodidact') he has met at the library, and perfunctory couplings with the landlady of a local bar. The 'incidents' that occur are few and far between: a visit to the local art gallery; lunch with the auto-didact; sex with the landlady; research for his book; a meeting in Paris with an old flame, Anny; the abandonment of the Rollebon biography; a traumatic encounter with a chestnut tree in the local park . . . the decision to leave Bouville and return to Paris. The action, such as it is, takes place outside of Roquentin, whose attitude throughout is that of the silent observer, studying the vain agita-tion of a world from which he feels increasingly alienated.

The diary form itself is, of essence, episodic, separating lived experience into self-contained parcels bounded by the arbitrary divisions of the calendar. And yet, if one defines 'plot' as the deferred resolution of an enigma, then something resembling a plot exists in *La Nausée*, for all its deceptive formlessness. The first diary entry begins: 'Something has happened to me, I can no longer doubt that.'[28] Something has changed 'But where . . . is it me that has changed?'[29] The keeping of the diary is motivated by the desire to keep track of this change and, eventually, perhaps, to understand it: 'The best thing would be to write down what happens daily. To keep a diary in order to understand it.'[30] The symptom of Roquentin's malaise is a feeling of nausea that has been assailing him with increasing frequency and which initially appears to be linked to objects. A pebble that is dry on one side and slimy on the other; a fork; a door handle; a person's hand that metamorphoses into a flaccid white maggot; a pair of mauve braces that cannot decide whether they want to be red or blue; the bench-seat in a tram; a piece of muddy scrap-paper lying by a puddle . . . In this way, Roquentin's malaise is presented to us like the corpse in the drawing room; the enigma is: who- or what-dunnit? It is no accident if *La Nausée* resembles a metaphysical detective story. Sartre and Beauvoir were great aficionados of detective fiction; indeed, it was largely thanks to Beauvoir that Sartre had been persuaded to abandon the original, stilted narrative form of his

'factum' and to 'spice it up' with intrigue, sex and suspense. True to
the genre, there are red herrings in this mystery: different possible
culprits fall under suspicion, only to be released by the narrator
for lack of evidence. Suspicion falls first on the *subject*: 'I think it
is me that has changed: that is the simplest solution.'[31] Perhaps
Roquentin's solitary lifestyle, coupled with the fact that he had
always been 'subject to brusque transformations' is sufficient
explanation in itself? But on reflection Roquentin is more
inclined to situate the blame outside of himself, in the *object*: 'It
was a kind of sickly sweet feeling . . . and it was coming from the
pebble. I am sure of it, it was passing from the pebble into my
hands.'[32] For much of the novel, there is a hesitation, a fluctuation,
a coming-and-going between these two positions, before a third
possibility is introduced. This also concerns the subject–object
dichotomy, but here the subject is consciousness and the object
the physical body. In a particularly virulent attack of nausea,
following his abandonment of the biographical project, the non-
philosopher Roquentin discovers for himself the old Cartesian
mind–body dualism: 'Me, the body: it lives all by itself once it's
started. But I'm the one who prolongs my thought . . . my
thought is me: that's why I can't stop, I exist because I think . . .
and I can't stop myself from thinking.'[33] If the body is *both* an
object in the world *and* the object that I exist, then nausea must
reside not at one or other pole, but in the *relation* between the
two poles of lived experience. Roquentin's nausea, it is now
revealed, is nothing more than the taste of himself: 'there's frothy
water in my mouth. I swallow it, it slides down my throat, it
strokes me – and there it is back in my mouth again . . . And that
little pool of water is me too. And the tongue. And the throat:
all me!'[34] But the mystery is not yet fully elucidated; at the climax
of all good whodunnits comes the naming of the culprit, and
Roquentin has not yet succeeded in *putting a name* to the cause of
his malaise. This revelation is delayed for a further 40 pages, and

it takes place not before the suspects assembled in the drawing room but before the mute and massive presence of a chestnut tree in the local park. As Roquentin, already in the throes of an attack of nausea, contemplates the tree, the scales abruptly fall from his eyes: 'Suddenly, existence had unveiled itself.'[35] The names we give to things, the uses we put them to, the categories we place them in are but 'faint marks that men have traced on their surface'.[36] Remove these traces and what remains is the meaning of existence, and the meaning of existence is, precisely, that it has none. Anything and anybody could disappear from this world and it would remain just as full as it was before: 'None of us had the slightest reason to be there. Each existent felt embarrassed, vaguely anxious, somehow excessive or 'in the way' [*de trop*] in relation to all the others'.[37] 'De trop' is the first term that occurs to Roquentin to describe our existence; a little later another occurs to him: 'The word Absurdity now comes to life under my pen.'[38] 'Absurd' is closer but not quite there: 'I'm struggling with words . . . Oh! How could I pin that down with words?'[39] Still too close to the overwhelming lived experience, Roquentin is incapable of conceptualizing it, but, when reflecting on it a little later, the task appears easier:

> To be honest, I wasn't really formulating my discovery. But now I think it would be easy to put it into words. The essential thing is contingency. What I mean is that existence is not, by definition, necessity . . . there were people who understood that, I think. Only they tried to surmount this contingency by inventing a necessary being that was its own cause. But no necessary being can explain existence.[40]

So there we are finally: the villain of the piece was contingency all along! The irony being that it is the unmasking of contingency that imparts *necessity* to every word of the narrative.

All the other themes of the novel depend on the intuition of contingency, and two of them are of particular importance, as they go right to the heart of Sartre's relation to writing and, more generally, the creative act. Beauvoir reports that Sartre's thought on necessity and contingency had first crystallized through an aesthetic experience: 'It was as he watched the images on a cinema screen that he had had the revelation of the necessity of art and had discovered, by an effect of contrast, the deplorable contingency of things in the world.'[41] While Sartre himself had 'intuited' contingency in the contrast between life and the images of a movie, Roquentin makes this discovery whilst listening to music. As he slumps over his beer in the *Rendez-vous des cheminots*, a record comes on the gramophone; it is *Some of these Days*, a well-known jazz-blues song. As the refrain approaches, he thinks 'it seems inevitable, so strong is the necessity of this music'.[42] And, magically, his nausea subsides, as if vanquished by this dose of sheer necessity. Roquentin is yearning for a life of rigorous necessity: 'what summits could I not reach if my *own life* was the substance of the tune'.[43] But melodies do not *exist* in this world; they simply *are*. As he listens one last time to the record, he fancies that he glimpses a possible connection. He starts to think of the composer of the song: He imagines a fat, sweating Jew, stuck in an apartment in a sweltering Brooklyn summer, beset with problems: money, women, health . . . but concludes: *he made that song*. And then he thinks of the singer – 'the Negress' – and concludes: 'The Jew and the Negress: those two are saved at least.'[44] From there, it is but a short step to wondering whether he, too, perhaps . . . 'It would have to be a book: that's all I know how to do.'[45] A book that would induce its readers to think of him in precisely the way that he thinks of the creators of *Some of these Days*. But how, exactly, does he think of them? If he brings them back to life, it is through a combination of biographical and fictionalizing impulses. On the one hand he states that 'I'd like to know a few things about that guy'; on the other, he freely embroiders

– or fictionalizes – on an empty canvas: the 'life' of the 'Jew' in 'Brooklyn' is pure fiction. A fiction, interestingly enough, of Sartre's creation, not Roquentin's: *Some of these Days* was actually written by a black Canadian composer called Shelton Brooks, and sung by a white, Jewish singer, Sophie Tucker. If Sartre supposes it to have been the other way round, it is probably because his own imagination has followed the groove of a well-worn cliché of the Jazz Age: the Jewish composer and the black singer. In any case, fiction prevails: 'For me they are . . . a bit like heroes in a novel; they've cleansed themselves of the sin of existing.'[46] So salvation for Roquentin would consist in being transformed into 'a hero in a novel' by his future readers.

Any reader of existing biographies of Sartre, of Beauvoir's memoirs or of the heavily annotated Pléiade edition of the *Œuvres romanesques* will be aware of the myriad points of contact between the real life of Sartre and the fictional life of Roquentin. When he wrote in *Les Mots* 'I *was* Roquentin, I showed in him, quite dispassionately, the very texture of my life',[47] he was no doubt intending to echo Flaubert's famous 'Mme Bovary, c'est moi', and it is a no less problematic claim. On the face of it, Sartre appears to have deliberately multiplied the dissimilarities with his protagonist, but these differences are entirely superficial, given that the 'texture' of their lives is supposedly identical. Most importantly, both produce *texts*, and it is in the way they relate to the activity of writing that the nature and limits of the identification must be sought. They are writers of different kinds. Roquentin is a dilettante, a 'Sunday writer'. The writing of the Rollebon biography was not driven by necessity, and there is no indication that writing had ever played an important part in Roquentin's previous existence. Sartre, on the other hand, lived in order to write: writing had been the fundamental activity of his life since childhood. 'Fundamental' in the strong sense of the word: writing was the very foundation on which his life had been constructed: everything else was subordinated to it. It is only when Roquentin's life starts to crumble about him, and he fears for his sanity, that writing – for him too – becomes a matter of life and death. He notes in his diary: 'The truth is, I'm afraid to let go of my pen.'[48] It is writing, in the physical sense of tracing letters on a page, that staves off nausea: every day, Roquentin awakens to a blank page, the blankness signifying that nothing ever happens *and* that *anything* could happen. Writing gives a sense (direction) to that page, even if it is only the left to right and top to bottom of his cursive script: writing takes place between death and madness, between the blankness of banality and the unbridled phantasmagoria that threaten to fill that blank. Sartre's daily existence might have been as nauseatingly contingent as the next man's, but this was compensated by the fact that his *life* had a shape. He had a vocation. He did not need to choose between 'living' and 'recounting': his life story was *already written*: had he not been living out the life of the Great Writer ever since he fell victim to the biographical illusion as a child?

La Nausée was widely reviewed and the praise was lavish and virtually unanimous. A few dissenting voices were 'nauseated' by its dark vision of the world; others – more perspicacious – criticized the 'whiff of the philosophy teacher' that hung over the text. But most were enthusiastic, heralding 'one of our greatest novelists', an 'enormous talent', a 'French Kafka', etc.[49] In fact, when *La Nausée* was published, Sartre's name was already known to the literary *cognoscenti* of Paris, if not yet to a wider reading public: the prestigious *Nouvelle Revue Française* had already published four of his short stories, starting in July 1937.

In many ways, the short stories represent a more startling achievement than the novel: the latter had been written and rewritten over a period of eight years, whereas the short stories seemed to spring from nowhere. If the novel had been formally innovative – so much so that many have seen it as a forerunner of the *nouveau roman* – the short stories demonstrate a virtuosic mastery of the conventions of the genre. There are several common strands in the five stories of *Le Mur*. One of these is a preoccupation with pathological psychology. This was not new: Sartre had been as interested in psychology as he was in philosophy at the ENS; he had made several visits to psychiatric hospitals, including one in 1936 that is recounted in grizzly detail by Beauvoir in her memoirs; his bad experience with mescaline and the power of his obsession with Olga had given him grounds to question his own mental stability. The theme of madness underlies virtually all of his work, and is particularly explicit in the later theatre, but it undergoes considerable modification over the years. In *Les Mots*, he goes so far as to suggest that a certain insanity is a defining characteristic of what it is to be human; in the early works he was more concerned with the question of whether madness involved an external modification of consciousness, or whether it was, in a sense, 'chosen' by the subject. The problem was of central importance to the radically anti-deterministic theory of consciousness that he had been trying to elaborate for many years. He was convinced that freedom is the defining characteristic of 'human reality', that our every action is freely chosen as a function of the 'fundamental choice we make of ourselves'. He was equally convinced that deterministic explanations of human behaviour were, at heart, attempts to deny an uncomfortable truth: if we are free, we are also totally responsible for our acts and their consequences. Clearly, 'madness' poses a problem for this theory: does an unfortunate soul in the advanced stages of dementia *choose* his madness? Sartre could easily have sidestepped the problem by invoking notions of normality and abnormality, so freedom would hold good for 'normal' subjects but not for subjects whose mental functioning was in some sense abnormal. But such was Sartre's radicality that he chose instead to see the very opposition between normality and abnormality as part of the problem, rather than the solution to it. The question is broached in the short story titled 'La chambre', where the aetiology of Pierre's premature dementia is clearly physiological, whilst the *specific content* of his delirium is clearly analysable in psychological terms.

Two of the other stories also concern pathological psychology: 'Intimité' deals with a 'case' of female frigidity, and 'Erostrate' has as its narrator-protagonist a sociopath who derives sexual pleasure from the humiliation of prostitutes and who aims to gain post-humous notoriety by embarking on a random killing spree in the streets of Paris.

In his brief preface to the collection, Sartre wrote: 'Nobody wants to face up to Existence. Here are five little routs in the face of Existence – some tragic, some comic – five lives.'[50] For 'Existence' read 'Contingency': to exist is, as we have seen, to exist without necessity or reason. But why, then, do we not all live our lives in a state of constant anxiety? From where do we draw the certainties that allow us to carry on? Sartre's answer is that we all have an intuitive comprehension, or 'grasp' of our contingency, but that we avoid confronting, and therefore 'assuming' this state of affairs by employing a range of evasive strategies that he calls *mauvaise foi* (bad faith). Beauvoir tells us that he had 'forged' this notion in the 1930s initially to account for the apparent manifestations of the Freudian unconscious (a notion that he found philosophically nonsensical). Each of the stories in *Le Mur* involves characters who are in bad faith and who try to run away from existence. Thus Lulu, in 'Intimité' succeeds in doing precisely what she pro-foundly *wants* to do, whilst persuading other people, *and herself*, that she is doing it against her will. She makes Fate or Force of Circumstance responsible for her own choices: 'You get caught in the current and carried off, that's life; you can't judge, or understand, you just have to let yourself go with the flow.'[51] Her self-deception is neither unconscious nor fully conscious: it inhabits the region described by Sartre as 'pre-reflexive'.

Bad faith is not only applicable to individual psychology: it can define the conduct and attitudes of whole social groups. This much was already evident from the savage presentation of the bourgeoisie in *La Nausée*. Bourgeois ideology has the effect of transforming historical contingency into eternal essence: the bourgeoisie is Good, Right, Normal, etc., *by definition*. But how does the bourgeoisie ensure the continuance of its hegemony? In other words, how does a child born into this class become what Sartre terms a *salaud* (a swine or bastard), convinced of his *right* to exist? The longest story in *Le Mur*, 'L'Enfance d'un chef', provides an answer. With a mixture of comic satire and burlesque, the story traces the development of Lucien Fleurier from infancy through to the 'mature' assumption of his rights and duties as a solid citizen. From his preface, it is clear that Sartre sees Lucien as of the same breed as the *salauds* of *La Nausée*: 'Lucien Fleurier comes closest of all the characters to feeling that he exists, but he does not want that, he escapes, he takes refuge in the contemplation of his rights . . . '.[52] Given the worrying resemblances between Lucien's childhood and Sartre's own – as later described in *Les Mots* – a more intriguing question would be: How did Sartre avoid becoming a *salaud* himself? His answer would be that, unlike Lucien, he did not have a father . . .

Notwithstanding what has been said about the anti-bourgeois satire of these two early works, the truly political dimension is notable for its absence. In comparison, say, to the socialist realist novels written in the 1930s by Sartre's Communist friend Nizan, Sartre's novel and short stories are marked by predominantly literary and philosophical concerns. Readers of the preceding pages could have been left with the impression that the years between Sartre's graduation from ENS (1929) and the publication of *La Nausée* (1938) were tranquil and uneventful. In reality, they were amongst the most turbulent of the twentieth century. Mussolini's Fascists had been in power in Italy since the 1920s; Hitler came to power in Germany in 1933 – the year that Sartre spent in Berlin reading phenomenology. The effects of the Wall Street crash began to impact on a Europe that had initially thought itself immune.

Against a background of economic depression, mass unemployment and spiralling inflation and financial scandals, the *Front populaire* government had been formed in an attempt to head off what looked like the very real possibility of a Fascist coup in France – led by anti-democratic *ligues*, such as the Croix de Feu. In 1936 the Spanish Civil War began with the invasion by Franco's *falangistas*. As the British and French stood by and did nothing while Mussolini and Hitler openly supplied Franco's Fascists, workers, writers and intellectuals from all over Europe headed to Spain to fight to protect democracy. Throughout all of this, Sartre kept on writing. There were echoes of these events in the two early works (there is a brief mention of Communists and Nazis fighting in the streets of Berlin in *La Nausée*; Lucien Fleurier becomes a *camelot du roi* and ends up espousing the anti-Semitism of his class), but echoes is all they were. The fact is that Sartre, by his own admission, remained detached. He and Beauvoir may have been 'sympathetic' to the Front Populaire and to the Spanish republicans; they may have 'detested' the Fascists, but they *did* nothing, not even vote! Sartre felt that the philosopher should philosophize, the writer should write, and the writer-philosopher should remain steadfastly aloof from the vain agitations of the world. But that was about to change in the most dramatic of fashions.

International tension had been building steadily throughout the late 1930s and it came to a head in September 1938 with the so-called Munich crisis. German troops annexed the Sudetenland in Czechoslovakia, and, since the boundaries of that country had been formally guaranteed by Britain and France, it looked as though Europe was on the brink of war. In the event, war was postponed for a year when Hitler was appeased yet again as Chamberlain and Daladier 'sold out' the Czechs. The events of this last week of September 1938 are recounted in Sartre's 1945 novel, *Le Sursis*. As the title of the novel implies, all that was achieved in Munich was a temporary truce. Towards the end of August 1939 Sartre wrote to one of his girlfriends: 'Hitler can't possibly be really thinking about starting a war . . . it's a bluff.' But then two days later, to the same correspondent: 'So, stupidity has triumphed. I leave tonight at five o'clock.'[53] History can make fools of all of us.

We have no direct record of Sartre's reaction when he learnt that he was called up, but one could imagine a reaction similar to that of Mathieu Delarue, the hero of *Le Sursis*: '"Category 2, but that's me!" Suddenly, it was as if the poster was targeting him; it was as if someone had written his name on the wall in chalk, with insults and threats.'[54] For the first time in life, Sartre found himself interpellated by history.

On 2 September 1939, he reported for duty with the 70th Division in Nancy. And thus began nineteen months that were to change his life for ever.

2

Of Arms and a Man

Speaking in 1975 Sartre was in no doubt as to the personal significance of the war years: 'The clearest thing about my life is that there was a break which means that there are two almost entirely separate moments . . . before the war, and after.'[1] Most people who lived through World War II understandably saw it as a break dividing their life into a 'before' and an 'after', but Sartre is claiming that the schism was so radical that the later Sartre hardly recognized himself in the earlier one.

Objectively, the change could not have been more brutal: from the cultural capital of the world, he is suddenly transported to a succession of sleepy Alsatian villages: Marmoutier, Brumath, Morsbronn, Bouxwiller. Transported also in time, back to a past that was 'his' although he had never personally experienced it: the region was the home of his maternal family, the Schweitzers. Having surrounded himself in Paris with a coterie of admiring female friends and lovers, he now found himself in the most aggressive of male environments. In effect, Sartre had spent his life to that point immersed in various elites – whether as a trainee member of the elite (at the ENS), as an educator of the future elite (at the *lycée*) or as a producer of entertainments for the elite (chez Gallimard). Now, he was simply Sartre, infantryman second-class attached to the meteorological corps. He found himself forced to coexist with men from quite different social backgrounds and horizons: an employee of the French telephone company, a Parisian

Jew who worked in the rag-trade, and a provincial schoolteacher. As we saw, Mathieu Delarue – the hero of the novel that Sartre was working on at this moment – initially experiences his 'call-up' as a somewhat unpleasant nomination, but at least it saves him from total anonymity: 'Here we go, I'm starting to become interesting.'[2] Sartre, however, had already begun to 'make a name for himself' in the literary and artistic circles of pre-war Paris. Little surprise, then, that his trajectory is the opposite of Mathieu's: he finds himself plunged back into anonymity: initially, at least, nobody knows *who* he is – his life is worth no more or less than that of the comrades he calls his 'acolytes'. Dispensable, replaceable, interchangeable: he becomes just anyone. The experience of belonging to a *mass* – anathema to the elitist Sartre of the pre-war period – will later be identified by Sartre as one of the most important discoveries of his life.

By all accounts, Sartre and his acolytes were not overburdened by military duties; their work consisted in releasing a balloon twice a day, observing its flight, and performing a few simple calculations to obtain wind speed and direction. The rest of the day they were free. Sartre employed this leisure to good effect: he continued to do precisely what he always had done – namely, to read and to write, enormously. Whereas most soldiers might write to their loved ones to send them razor-blades, chocolate or tobacco, Sartre demanded books (and the odd pouch of tobacco, admittedly). He read everything from Heidegger to second-rate detective novels; everything from Pepys's diary to those of Gide, Dabit and Renard. He read histories of World War I and analyses of the rise of Nazism, as though attempting, finally, to understand how he came to be where he was. He read philosophy and biographies (one of his long-standing fascinations). He read history and novels. He often read for twelve hours a day until his one good eye 'flickered and went out' (a childhood illness had left Sartre virtually blind in his right eye since the age of four). And he wrote. To reflect on the

sheer volume of writing that Sartre produced during the nine
months of the Phoney War is to be confronted with an essential
truth: he was a machine for the production of text. The daily letters
that he wrote to Beauvoir alone fill 500 pages of the *Lettres au
Castor*. He wrote and rewrote drafts of the thick novel that would
see the light of day in 1945 as *L'Age de raison*. Above all, he produced a war diary; the 1995 expanded edition of this diary is 600
pages long – and it contains only six of the fifteen notebooks that
he filled during this short period of ostensible 'inactivity'! With
the possible exception of the amphetamine-fuelled hyperactivity
of 1958–59, when he wrote the *Critique de la raison dialectique*,
these nine months must have been the most intensively literary
of Sartre's whole life. He wrote as if his life depended on it, and,
in more ways than one, it did.

Of all Sartre's posthumous publications, the *Carnets* are probably the most surprising and the most valuable for students of his
work; because of the manner and circumstances in which they were
produced, they take us to the very heart of his relation to writing.
Nowhere else does one grasp so forcefully what writing meant to
Sartre. When we read a diarist we witness the transformation and
the 'recycling' of the quotidian; we are aware that external events
are being transformed by a certain sensibility, for example, or by a
vision conditioned by class, or even by the pathology of the diarist.
All of these are present in the diaries, but the primary filter through
which the world is 'processed' and transformed is that of the intellect. To read the war diaries is to understand what it is to be an
intellectual – in the special sense of 'one who relates to the world
primarily through intellection' (as opposed to sensibility, physicality
etc.). It is a truism to say that everything is grist to the writer's mill,
but we are rarely given a glimpse of how that mill functions. What
is immediately striking about the diaries is the heteroclite nature of
the subject matter: they contain lengthy discussions of the books,
newspapers and reviews that Sartre is reading; reflections on the

progress of his novel; descriptions of his physical surroundings; often hilarious portraits of his 'acolytes' and their words and deeds; analyses of the 'military mentality', anguished speculation on what his girlfriend(s) back in Paris might be getting up to; a first, fragmented, autobiographical sketch; an early attempt at 'existential psychoanalysis'; many pages of dense philosophical analysis. And all of this is woven into the weft and warp of the everyday absurdities of life as a soldier in this 'Kafkaesque war'.

His oft-repeated claim that the war had 'changed' him, that the experience of comradeship, captivity and occupation had 'transformed' him from aloof individualist into activist, would have been accepted as self-evident, had it not been for the posthumous publication of the diaries. *Objectively*, these claims are unquestionable in any case: one has only to compare what Sartre did and wrote before the war to what he did and wrote after it. But what the diaries do is to allow us to witness the process of change and its vicissitudes; to ask ourselves what changed and what remained the same, and, above all, to reflect on the role played by *writing* in this self-transformation: the diaries are, at one and the same time, the record of a transformation and the supposed means by which it is brought about. If one examines the various functions that writing performed for Sartre at this moment, one is led into the heart of the artist's relation to his medium.

Like most conscripts, Sartre's first reaction to the situation was a feeling of disorientation and loss of autonomy. Not surprising, then, that the first function of the daily practice of writing was to help the writer gain his bearings, or 'reorientate' himself and reassert his illusory independence. At a moment when the 'outside' (other people, the possibility of death, the military hierarchy, the intentions of the enemy) was oppressively important and threatened to overwhelm or invade the 'inside', writing was a means of reasserting the prerogatives of interiority. It is striking in this respect that the first notebook – covering the first six weeks at the front – should be almost entirely devoted to topics such as the 'world of war' – as if this act of intellectualization was a means of magically establishing the subject's control of this world whose first characteristic was, precisely, that it robbed the individual of control and personal identity.

This desire to maintain control is particularly evident where other people are concerned. In order to understand this, one has to remember that these notebooks were anything but a personal diary. Although Sartre was unsure as to whether they would be fit for a general public, he wrote with a particular public in mind: when completed, they were taken or sent back to Beauvoir, who then circulated them amongst the intimate group of the 'family' – primarily Bost, Olga and Wanda. Knowing precisely who would read them doubtless enabled Sartre to calculate their effect. In this respect they were similar to the many letters he wrote to Beauvoir, Wanda, and others. Before September 1939 he had held court amidst a coterie of female friends, controlling this network and the flow of information within it with cynical efficiency. Now he is removed to a distance of several hundred kilometres and placed uncomfortably at the end of a somewhat aleatory line of communication. Writing now became the only means of maintaining control over what he called his 'cardinal points'. This particular function of writing is thrown into relief by two incidents which saw him losing control over his interlocutors, then regaining it through the power of his pen.[3]

The ultimate invasion of the inside by the outside is death itself: '[death is] the presence of the outside in the very heart of my self.'[4] Even if death was not a probability – given that Sartre was not a front-line soldier – it was at least a possibility, and this forced him to reflect on its meaning. Characteristically, he regards death as the absurd interruption of a *narrative*. On occasions, this narrative takes the pictorial form of a pre-sketched embroidery cloth just waiting to be filled in (nowadays one would think more of 'painting by numbers'); at other times this narrative is a journey: 'I now realize that I set off in life as if I was commencing a long journey, but a journey of a given distance and with a fixed destination. I must arrive at my destination before nightfall.'[5] And writing is not simply one of the motifs of the embroidery, or one of the incidents along the way: it is the very form and content of everything. He had thought of his life and his *œuvre* as being co-extensive with his life – with, admittedly, a slice of 'non-life' at the beginning and the end (infancy and senility): 'I have always conceived of my writings not as isolated productions but as being organised into an *œuvre*. And this œuvre was contained within the limits of a human life.'[6] We can thus arrive at a series of propositions: the daily practice of writing (*écriture*) produces writings (*écrits*), and writings produce an *œuvre*; this *œuvre* will only be complete if fitted into a 'normal' lifespan; *therefore*, as long as the *œuvre* is in progress (that is, as long as the writings are being produced by the daily practice of writing) death cannot logically intervene. That is, it is writing that constantly defers the untimely arrival of death. Like a latterday Scheherezade, Sartre talks/writes to stay alive. It is in the light of this that we may understand the terms in which he describes his fanatical attachment to the completion of his journey: 'I do not wish to feel my tiredness or to stop. My entire will is straining towards the goal. There is no place for lassitude or diversion, I never let myself go, everything is a function of this journey.'[7] This was the necessity that drove him to write for up to twelve hours a day during the Phoney War. With death lying in wait, perhaps, just over the horizon, he would have said, like Roquentin: 'The truth is that I am afraid to let go of my pen.' Writing is his talisman: 'I haven't got time to die . . . Magically, that provides me with the certainty that I will not die before I have arrived at the end of my journey.'[8] The objection that he was simply writing to 'kill time' is in fact less an objection than a confirmation. As he writes, he removes himself from real time (in which men live and die): time is converted into space, and that space is measured by the accumulation of letters and words, and phrases and lines, and pages and notebooks . . . This spatialization of time is discernible on many occasions in the war diaries. On 27 March 1940, for example, he writes, as though wistfully recalling an ancient aberration: 'It is a long time now since I worried about authenticity or about Nothingness.'[9] In fact, a mere two weeks previously he had written a long entry on precisely those subjects, but the two entries are separated from each other by the 'time' of 17,000 words of text. As he himself remarks: 'I have always regarded abundance as a virtue!'[10]

The characters in Sartre's 1944 play *Huis clos* are placed in a hell containing no mirrors, thus condemning them to seek their own image forever in each other's eyes. The situation is not unlike that of Sartre in the autumn of 1939: deprived of the defining gaze of his faithful entourage, he is surrounded by men who have not yet learned how to see him. He becomes, in a sense, invisible. Predictably, his writings become his mirror. Although the second notebook is missing, we know that in it he began to write a self-portrait at the start of November of that year. This early autobiographical sketch (it continues in the other notebooks) is one of the most original aspects of the *Carnets*. If the diaries resemble a fabric woven from many different strands, the self-portrait is just one strand amongst many – appearing sometimes on the surface, at other times hidden behind more prominent strands of the narrative, but ever-present. While providing a wealth of 'factual' information about the first 34 years of his life, the sketch is not ordered as a chronological narrative: the organization is thematic and episodic, with life-themes being prompted partly by events of the moment, and partly by the philosophical speculations that run through the text. In this way, we learn details about different periods of Sartre's life by way of illustration of themes such as fame, glory, death, relations with others, sex, friendship, property, ownership, money. This fragmented, thematic approach to life-writing could well have been inspired by Michel

Leiris's *L'Age d'homme*, which Sartre had just read with interest.[11] What it illustrates above all, however, is the inseparability of the various strands of Sartre's reflections. When he remarks that 'life and philosophy are henceforth one and the same thing',[12] we are able fully to understand the resonances of that claim.

For those of us who approached Sartre's life first through *Les Mots*, only later to discover the *Carnets*, reading the latter is a disquieting experience. This is not because of the differences in the accounts but because of their uncanny similarity, right down to the level of verbal formulations. In light of this, it is all the more surprising that he gives change as the motivation for keeping his diary:

> I abhorred personal diaries and I thought that man is not made to see himself, that he should keep his eyes fixed straight ahead. I have not changed. But I think, on the occasion of some grand circumstance or other, and when one is in the process of changing one's life, like the snake sloughing off its skin, that one can look at this dead skin, at this brittle image of a snake that one has left behind, and see where one is now.[13]

The intention is clearly to 'sum up', then to move on. The final word on this stock-taking exercise comes some five months later – in March 1940 – and it is not self-indulgent: 'I have no solidarity with anything, not even with myself; I do not need anybody or anything. This is the character that I have created for myself over the last thirty-four years . . . I have no liking for this character and I want to change.'[14] Curiously, he appears to be further from effecting this change at the end of the diaries than he was at the beginning: they start with 'I am changing' and end with 'I want to change'. In between come numerous affirmations that this change has already occurred. Matters are further complicated by the nature of this 'character' that he identifies as 'me'. The problem takes the form of a logical paradox, or a riddle: 'what is the creature that is not what it is, and is what it is not?' The 'me' that must change and be left behind is the 'me' whose defining characteristic is this very tendency to self-repudiation. As Sartre himself admits, to identify and denounce a character trait is not sufficient, in itself, to change it. Only an idealist could have such faith in the magical-performative value of mere words. All of this raises the question of the possibility of change, or of the relevance of the question 'what changes and what remains the same?'

The fact remains that an *objective* change was effected between 1939 and 1945: the 'abstract man of the plutodemocracies' emerges as the socially committed intellectual. Underlining once more the interdependence of the various strands running through the *Carnets*, this theme of change is played out through an extended reflection on a particular *philosophical* notion. The notion in question is authenticity, but Sartre was always more adept at exposing the inauthentic than he was at defining the authentic. Already in the short story 'Le mur' he had engaged with the notion of authenticity in relation to death. Taking issue with Heidegger's idea of 'Being-towards-Death' – the idea that death is our 'ownmost possibility', as Heidegger put it – Sartre had suggested in that story that, far from being the culmination towards which our existence is constantly directed, death is rather the irruption of absurdity into the heart of a life: rather than being the final note in a concerto that resolves everything that has gone before, it is more like the roof collapsing on the head of the pianist: one always dies too early, or too late, but never 'on time'. At this moment (1939–40) Sartre is faced for the first time with the possibility of his own 'premature' death. Many of the early entries in the diaries are concerned with the attitude he should strike in the face of this eventuality: stoic detachment or a wailing and gnashing of teeth. But he is in fact more interested in life than in death: 'life' defined as the accretion of spent choices, as the network of relations and activities that one builds over time, and that one comes to identify as oneself. The war is a point of rupture, but a rupture that can be positive or negative, depending on the attitude one adopts to it. There is no doubt that Sartre initially hoped that the war would be brief – a mere parenthesis in the midst of his life – and that his life would continue unchanged before too many months. His 'life', as he makes clear, is the carapace he had formed for himself: his friends and lovers, his literature and his philosophy, his job, his habits (he was, perhaps surprisingly, a creature of quite rigid habits). But running counter to this is the temptation to throw everything over, to renounce everything and everyone, to smash the mould and recast himself in a different image: 'I have a real inferiority complex vis-à-vis Gauguin, Van Gogh and Rimbaud, because they were able to lose themselves . . . I'm more and more sure that, to achieve authenticity, something has to snap.'[15] But what? Gauguin had quit his job and abandoned wife and family to pursue his art; Van Gogh had gone mad. But Rimbaud was the most radical: proclaimed a genius while still a teenager, he had *stopped writing* at the age of twenty and simply turned himself into something else. Sartre was convinced that such decisions could not have been the result of reflection, but must have been taken spontaneously, in a violent revolution of the whole personality. And these are the alternatives that shape his thought in the *Carnets*: reflection or spontaneity; self-repetition or radical transformation.

A second Heideggerian notion – historicity – comes together with authenticity and helps to bring the choice into focus. To embrace historicity, in Sartre's case, meant relinquishing the social and political aloofness of the pre-war years. It involved realizing and acting upon a simple observation: no man is an island complete unto himself; our being is irremediably social and historical. So any conversion to authenticity must also involve drawing the consequences of one's historicity.

As Sartre was well aware, it is one thing to grasp the nature of the transformation that must be wrought, but quite another to bring it about, especially when one is 'thirty-four years old and cut-off from everything, like an air-plant.'[16] In the midst of grappling with his own 'conversion', Sartre was also writing the first volume of what would become *Les Chemins de la liberté*, whose protagonist, Mathieu, is faced with the selfsame dilemma. Stuck in a job that no longer motivates him, trapped in a relationship that is a bourgeois marriage in all but name, losing hair and gaining kilos, Mathieu – like Sartre – does not like the 'character' he has created for himself. The siren voices of change are there: should he settle for the bourgeois respectability offered by his brother? Or the life of political commitment that makes his friend Brunet appear so strong and solid? Or perhaps he should kick over the traces and declare his passion for the volatile, unpredictable, and much younger, Ivich? In the end he does nothing. Paralysed by an excess of reflexivity, he will never 'lose himself' because he is afraid to close his eyes and take the plunge. The Spanish civil war had passed him by, so had the Popular Front: he remained 'free for all commitments, but knowing that one must never commit oneself'.[17] But what use was his freedom? At the end of the first volume, he reflects bitterly that his freedom has simply been 'absorbed' by his life, like ink by blotting-paper.

Meanwhile, Mathieu's creator seemed to be moving confidently beyond his character's predicament. In a letter to the editor Brice Parain in February 1940, Sartre is in pugnacious, if individualistic, form: 'As far as politics are concerned, don't worry: I will go into that brawl alone, I will follow no one and those who want to follow me will follow me.'[18] An entry in the diaries from early March suggests that he still has some way to go, but at least he knew where he *should* be going: 'Le Castor [Beauvoir] writes me that true authenticity does not consist in overflowing one's life on all sides or in standing back from it to judge it, or freeing oneself from it at every moment, but rather in plunging into it and becoming one with it.'[19] Authenticity means acting in and on the world and then being one with those acts – not disowning them as having been committed by another 'me' who has been left behind, sloughed off like a snake's skin. He finds an image to describe this tendency of his to avoid responsibility for his actions and to eschew engagement in the real world – he calls it the 'tower of consciousness'. Indeed, more than a tendency, it is his very character. By mid-March 1940 he is preparing to descend from this tower forever, but this poses a fresh dilemma: if he relinquishes the airy refuge of the tower in order to ground himself in the world (to 'take root', as he puts it), will this not involve his becoming bogged-down in the world? Will he not fall into the dreaded 'spirit of seriousness': 'all serious thought is an abdication of man in favour of the world.'[20] His answer is a confident 'no': 'As authentic as one might be, one is no less free for all that – freer even than in the hypothesis of the tower – since one is condemned to a freedom without shadows and without excuses.'[21] This would-be authenticity, which surely prefigures the commitment of the post-war years, was not without its problems, however.

The most intractable problem concerns writing itself. Authentic commitment requires the individual to remove the safety-net and to put himself at risk in the world: the world outside the individual is a hazardous and unpredictable place, subject to laws that the individual has not created or, even worse, subject to the vagaries of random occurrence; only in the self-created inner world can the individual protect his autonomy and (illusory) omnipotence. Sartre is all too aware that the nature of his investment in writing is in fact a hindrance to the radical conversion to authentic living: 'Even in the war I fall on my feet because my immediate reflex is to write down what I feel and what I see. If I put myself into question, it is in order to write the results of that self-examination and of course I can see that I am merely *dreaming* of putting into question my desire to write.'[22] When he announces that he is ready to come down from his ivory tower, on the condition that his life remain a 'game', the contradiction is more than merely apparent: he is saying that he wants to act henceforth in the real world *and* continue to be defined by an activity (writing) that is the very negation of reality.

This contradiction is at the heart of an important text published in February 1940. *L'Imaginaire*, which followed on directly from *L'Imagination*, was the culmination of work on the nature of the image begun as early as the 1920s, and inspired by Husserlian phenomenology. Sartre argues that consciousness can project itself towards its intentional objects in two fundamental ways: perception and imagination. When I perceive an object, I posit it as real and present; if I imagine it, I am positing it as unreal and absent. Consciousness cannot simultaneously imagine and perceive an object. This radical and contentious theory creates an absolute divorce between the real and the imaginary. Unfortunately, it also drives a wedge between the ethical and the aesthetic: 'The real is never beautiful . . . That is why it is stupid to confuse ethics and aesthetics.'[23] As Sartre had already suggested in *La Nausée*, only circles, squares, melodies, works of art etc. have necessity; the real world is governed by contingency and absurdity.

As the Phoney War dragged on through the spring of 1940, Sartre was clearly not yet ready to take this plunge into the 'heart of existence', and 'everything that is most contingent and absurd about it'. Of course, if writing could somehow be considered as *action in the world*, then the contradiction would be resolved . . .

In the third volume of *Les Chemins de la liberté*, the 'Mathieu cycle' comes to an end and the 'Brunet cycle' begins. Encircled by the rapidly advancing German forces, Mathieu makes an absurd gesture towards freedom by opting to stay and fight with some front-line soldiers atop a bell-tower, in a futile attempt to slow the enemy advance. At the very moment when the tower (clearly an echo of Sartre's own 'ivory tower') collapses under the German mortars, Brunet – the Communist activist – calmly emerges from the cellar where he had been billeted and gives himself up: for him, the struggle was only just beginning. The circumstances of Sartre's own capture were as anticlimactic as those of Brunet: retreating through Hagenau and Breschwillers, he was taken prisoner without firing a shot in a small village called Padoux, near Epinal. It was 21 June 1940: his thirty-fifth birthday. After spending two months in a holding camp at Baccarat, he was transferred in mid-August to Stalag XIID at Trier in Germany, near the border with Luxembourg. It is during the eight months of the Stalag that Sartre himself situates the break between 'before' and 'after'. In this city of 25,000 men, insulated from the war, with its inescapable promiscuity, its social hierarchies, its cliques and cabals, its everyday currency of schemes and scams, Beauvoir's words must have come back to Sartre: 'It is *beyond* the crowd . . . that one is alone. Whereas I affirmed my solitude *against* the crowd.'[24] After spending a few weeks in the relative comfort of the infirmary, Sartre's malingering was uncovered and he was sent to the 'Artists' Hut'. But his closest associates – by dint of intellectual affinity, rather than religious leaning – were the chaplains and priests, of whom there were a great many in the camp, many of them highly educated Jesuits. Against all probability, he was happy in this collective existence. Those who had known the morose, aggressive recluse of the Phoney War – always buried in his books – must have been surprised by the change that came over him in the camp. Unlike the Phoney War, this was a black and white world, a world of them and us in which 'they' were brutally visible and visibly brutal: the presence of the enemy served both to unite the prisoners and to flatten out the differences that would have been apparent in peace-time: 'What I liked in the camp was the feeling of being part of the mass. There was a seamless communication, day and night, when we talked to each directly, as equals. That taught me a lot.'[25]

At Christmas 1940 Sartre had his first experience of how art might function in the service of the masses; he undertook to write, produce and direct, in a mere six weeks, a Nativity play, of all things. In fact, beneath the cover of the Nativity, the play was a call to resistance. The eponymous hero, Bariona, is the leader of a national liberation movement, vowed to throw the Romans out of Judea. The message was clear enough – even if it did go apparently unnoticed by the watching German guards: freedom or death, hope in the face of the most hopeless odds. The importance of the play does not reside in its modest literary merits, but in what Sartre learnt from the experience. This is summed up in a text published after the Liberation, in English: 'It was then, as I spoke to my comrades across the footlights about their situation as prisoners, seeing them suddenly so remarkably silent and attentive, that I realised what the theatre should be – a great, collective religious phenomenon.'[26] Sartre would relive this experience many times over the next twenty years: it was to be his plays – not his novels, his philosophical treatises, or even his journalism – that would bring his ideas directly to the public, in France and all over the world.

So happy was Sartre with the new life he had found in the Stalag, that when the opportunity arose for him to escape, he only did so with a certain reluctance. In March 1941 he was released thanks to a forged medical certificate stating that he was unfit for active service, due to his semi-blindness.

The Sartre who returned to Paris on 12 April 1941 was – outwardly at least – a changed man. Beauvoir was taken aback by the transformation, shocked by the 'inflexibility of his moralizing attitude'. The 'unanimous life' of the Stalag had left a deep mark in him: henceforth, 'salvation' was to be sought in action. But what kind of action? Occupied Paris was not the Manichaean world of the Stalag. If Sartre had 'lost his bearings' during the Phoney War, then occupied France of spring 1941 was an even more disorientating place. Sartre's natural milieu – that of the intellectual elite – was shattered and in disarray. Of the writers who had held centre stage in 1939, some had opted for collaboration, some had thrown in their lot with de Gaulle's Free French, others had subsided into

Sartre and Simone de Beauvoir in a Paris café, 1946–48.

despair or apathy, yet others had simply left on the last boat to the
USA. After the Hitler–Stalin pact of 1939, the Parti Communiste
Français (PCF) were stuck in a moral no-man's-land: viscerally hos-
tile to Fascism, but in a position of 'official' collaboration with the
Nazis. All publications were subject to German or Vichy censorship.
But Sartre had returned to Paris in order to *act*, not to write.

The first manifestation of this desire was the formation, in
spring 1941, of a resistance group. The group initially consisted of
the 'family': Olga, Bost, Wanda, Jean Pouillon (another former pupil
from Le Havre) and their closest friends and colleagues. Sartre's and
Beauvoir's friend from ENS days, the philosopher Maurice Merleau-
Ponty, had already founded a small group of his own, and now the

two groups united under a single banner: *Socialisme et Liberté* (Socialism and Freedom). Made up entirely of teachers, lecturers, students and former pupils, the group had about 50 members. The programme was simple: to resist the Nazis, Vichy and collaboration in all its forms. The action they undertook was, perhaps, the only action that such a group could envisage: they wrote, printed and distributed seditious tracts calling for resistance against the occupier. In the summer of 1941, the group met to take stock of their situation. It was clear that, thus far, their action had been ineffectual. Some members of the group were losing patience and calling for more direct action; others wondered whether the risks they were running were not disproportionate to their achievements. Another problem lay in the difficulty of making contact with other groups. Paranoia was rife – for good reason – and established groups were wary of overtures from outsiders. The Communists, for their part, were spreading the rumour that Sartre had been freed from the Stalag due to the direct intervention of the collaborationist writer Drieu la Rochelle, and that he should be regarded as a German agent. This campaign was due in large part to Sartre's friendship with Paul Nizan. Nizan had been killed on 23 May 1940, but not before leaving the Party in disgust at the Hitler–Stalin pact: he was now the defenceless object of a PCF smear campaign.

In an attempt to make contacts and extend the activities of the group, Sartre and Beauvoir travelled to the *Zone libre* in summer 1941. The mission was a disaster. In André Gide, they met with an apathetic old man holed up in his villa on the Côte d'Azur; in André Malraux, they met with an opportunist waiting for the Russian tanks and American planes to win the war. In the event, notwithstanding his own self-aggrandizing account of events, the great *maquisard* Malraux did not actually enter the Resistance until early 1944.

It was a depressed Sartre that returned to Paris in autumn 1941 to take up a teaching post at the Lycée Condorcet. Socialism and

Freedom was in terminal decline; it staggered on until the end of the year before finally being disbanded. Like many other small, short-lived resistance groups of the first year of the occupation, it had foundered due to a lack of organized support, be it Gaullist or Communist. The most significant thing about the group was the programme embodied in its name: a truly collectivist socialism that nevertheless recognized and safeguarded the autonomy of each member of the collective. Sartre would devote the rest of his life to the pursuit of this implausible objective, in a variety of shapes and forms.

Sartre's first sally beyond the walls of the 'tower of consciousness' had resulted in a rebuff and a bloodied nose. It had proved more difficult than he might have imagined to 'take root' in the real world. In a characteristic movement, he withdrew to a place of safety. During 1942 he fell back on what he knew: writing. The energy that had failed to find a satisfactory outlet in active resistance appears to have been channelled back into writing. In little more than a year, working mainly in cafés (they, at least, were well-heated), he put the finishing touches to the first volume of *Les Chemins de la liberté*; commenced the second volume (*Le Sursis*); wrote a play (*Les Mouches*) and, astonishingly, wrote in its entirety *L'Etre et le néant* – the monumental volume on which his reputation as a philosopher is based. Almost by the bye, he also published important essays on Camus, Bataille and Blanchot whilst teaching full-time at the Lycée.

There is no doubt that, to Sartre's mind, every word he wrote after the failure of Socialism and Liberty was an *act* of resistance. This is illustrated particularly well by his first commercially performed play, *Les Mouches*. In an interview given after the Liberation of Paris, Sartre asserted that the play he had really wanted to write would have told the story of 'the terrorist who, by gunning down Germans in the street, provokes the execution of fifty hostages'.[27] Indeed, from the moment in August 1941 when a resistance fighter shot a German officer at Barbès métro station, the Nazi charm offensive was over: in September and October of that year, 100 hostages were murdered in reprisals.

Les Mouches was performed on 3 June 1943 at the Théâtre de la Cité, directed by and starring Charles Dullin. Like *Bariona*, the play was a form of what was known as 'contraband' literature: under the cover of a reworked Greek tragedy, Sartre's message of resistance was smuggled across the footlights to the audience. Returning to Argos, his birthplace, Oreste finds the throne usurped by Egisthe, who has murdered his father, the king, and taken his mother, Clytemnestre, as his wife. The power behind the throne is Jupiter himself. The Argives are kept in line by an official religion of remorse – devised by Jupiter and enforced by Egisthe. The parallels with Vichy were obvious enough. Since the armistice, Pétain had promoted just such a doctrine: if France had been defeated, it was because she had deserved it; now was the time to show appropriate remorse and guilt for the decadence and degeneracy that had so enfeebled the nation! But the play was far more than a circumstantial piece, limited by its historical context. Its subject is the one that was to become synonymous with Sartre: freedom. In murdering both the usurper *and* his mother – in defiance of received morality – and revindicating that act as good, Oreste liberates himself for a second time: he had arrived in Argos with an abstract freedom, suffering from an unbearable lightness of being; he departs bearing the guilt of the city on his shoulders. In the *Carnets*, Sartre had bemoaned his inability to ground himself in the world in a resonant phrase: 'I would have to be made of clay, instead I am made of wind.'[28] Oreste effects the transformation from 'wind' to 'clay'.

In terms of its political interpretation, the play probably raises more questions than it provides answers. Rather than remain and govern Argos as a free democracy, Oreste leaves its citizens to the tender mercies of his now remorseful sister Electre (who had assisted him in the murder) and Jupiter. One assumes that the Argives will simply resume their pattern of passive bad faith under the new old regime. The lack of political realism in Oreste's act (or was it a mere gesture?) and its idealistic individualism were traits that Oreste doubtless shared with Sartre himself, if this judgement on Socialism and Liberty by a former member is to be trusted:

> Right from the start they seemed puerile to me: for example, they never realized how much their empty chatter jeopardized the work done by others . . . And, although they may have learned certain reasoning techniques at University, I can tell you that when it came to political action they certainly didn't know how to reason.[29]

True or not, this opposition between the ineffectual chatter of intellectuals and the 'real' work performed by men of action would later be central to all of Sartre's major plays.

Les Mouches was a commercial failure; playing to poor houses, it was withdrawn after only twenty or so performances. Reviews in the collaborationist press were predictably hostile, although the venom was directed more at the aesthetics of the play than at any political 'message' that may have been detected. Nonetheless, *Les Mouches* brought Sartre back to a certain extent into the public eye, reminding readers of *La Nausée* and *Le Mur* that he still existed. Which is more than can be said for *L'Etre et le néant* when it was published in June 1943. Given the circumstances, it is unsurprising that the volume was noticed only by a handful of specialists. It was, as we will see, 'rediscovered' dramatically in 1945. Between 1943 and 1945 it appears to have served a more practical purpose: legend has it that the first edition weighed exactly one kilo, making it ideal for weighing out the rationed potatoes!

From spring 1943, Sartre's life started to change. He may have withdrawn into his creative shell in 1942, but the result of his vast labours had carried an image of him abroad, and a whole new network of contacts was taking shape without his even being aware of it. Popular flop it may have been, but *Les Mouches* brought Sartre's name to the attention of influential strangers. The filmmaker Jean Delannoy commissioned a screenplay from Sartre on the strength of what he had seen in his play; the writer and ethnographer Michel Leiris had written one of the few favourable reviews of the play, in the clandestine *Lettres françaises*. The sheer fact of being present on so many fronts – novel, short story, philosophy, theatre – served to broadcast Sartre's name and amplify his reputation. Moreover, in the incestuous circles of the Parisian *literati*, word of mouth was a formidable means of publicity. The authoritative articles of literary criticism published between 1939 and 1945 – first in the *Nouvelle Revue Française*, then in *Les Lettres Françaises* and the *Cahiers du Sud* – made him into a powerful arbiter of literary taste. They also opened unexpected doors. Sartre's glowing review of Albert Camus's debut novel, *L'Etranger*, led to Camus turning up and introducing himself at the dress rehearsal of *Les Mouches* in 1943.

As the occupation went from bad to worse – 1942, with its mass deportations of French Jewry, was the blackest year of all – Sartre went from strength to strength. In early 1943 the PCF decided to adopt a policy of inclusivity. Having slandered and denigrated Sartre, they now made overtures to him. With remarkably little bitterness, Sartre agreed to join the clandestine Comité National des Ecrivains (CNE). At the meetings of the CNE that he attended, Sartre enlarged his circle of new contacts still further: Gabriel Marcel, Paul Eluard, Michel Leiris, Raymond Queneau, Alberto Giacometti, François Mauriac (a celebrated Catholic novelist whom Sartre had criticized to devastating effect in an influential essay published in February 1939). From autumn 1943 Sartre and Beauvoir were caught in something resembling a social whirl. With the recent publication of her first novel (*L'Invitée*), Beauvoir, too, had joined the new literary elite. A famous photograph taken in spring 1944 encapsulates their life in the last year of the occupation.

Pablo Picasso had written a short play entitled 'Le désir attrapé par la queue' ('Desire caught by its tail/prick') and Michel and Zette Leiris decided to stage it in their flat, with their friends taking the leading roles. The snapshot – taken in Picasso's atelier – of the illustrious cast is eloquent in itself: surrounded, as always, by women, Picasso is the focal point (although he does not deign to look at the camera); Camus, with his dark good looks, is centre stage in the bottom row, confidently facing-down the camera; to his right, Leiris; to his left, Sartre. Sartre, too, is looking into the lens – inasmuch as his squint will permit him to. His position in the photograph – central but somehow also marginal, a part of the group, but apart from it – reflected his position within the artistic and intellectual elite of the moment: simultaneously inside and outside. With the Nazis suffering reversals on all fronts, thoughts were turning to a post-liberation France; Sartre's position was marked by ambivalence: 'State socialism and individual free-dom are opposed, that much is certain. But there are other forms of socialism . . .'.[30] He was perhaps naïve in the way he envisaged a 'third way' that would shun established parties and steer a path between them. However, this rejection of what *is*, in the name of what could be, is one of the constants of his thought: it had been there in his wholesale rejection of the hegemonic idealist philosophy of the ENS; it is there in *L'Etre et le néant*, in his theory of a 'nihilat-ing' consciousness summoning itself into being in an act of negation of what is; it is there in his rejection of Literature as an institution; it will be there, much later, in his critique of institutionalization in all its forms. It is there, perhaps most tellingly, in his perma-nent self-critique and his horror of sclerosis and inertia. For Sartre, any meaningful process of construction must commence with a questioning of what already is – simply *because* it already is.

On 27 May 1944 the Théâtre du Vieux-Colombier on the Left Bank was the scene of the literary event of the year: the première of Sartre's new play, *Huis clos*. This is perhaps his most perfect play: gone are the verbosity and epic pretensions of *Les Mouches*, to be replaced by a language and a situation that almost foreshadow Beckett in their economy. Three characters – a man and two women – are condemned to spend eternity together in a very Sartrean hell. Deprived of mirrors, they must rely on each other's gaze – and words – to maintain or create an image of themselves. Back in the land of the living, they have fallen forever into the public domain; henceforth, the living will decide who they *were*: Garcin the coward, Inès the lesbian, Estelle the infanticide. In hell, however, there is still everything to play for: to be 'saved', each must convince one of the others to see him/her as s/he wishes to be seen. But this is hell, after all, and things have been so arranged as to make this impossible: the characters will spend eternity searching for their own face. 'Hell is other people' exclaims Garcin – thus launching the first of many slogans by which a general public would come to 'know' Sartre. Anyone who *had* read *L'Etre et le néant* at the time would have known, however, that this was not intended as a universal judgement on human relations: the individual who relies *too much* on other people to know who he is does indeed place himself in a living hell: we must strike a balance between the objective knowledge that the Other possesses of us, and the less substantial subjective comprehension we may have of ourselves.

This particular balance was to prove difficult to maintain in Sartre's own case. *Huis clos* made of him something of a star: he was immediately in demand; requests rained down for interviews and texts; commissions and sundry other proposals arrived daily. From this moment on Sartre was constantly in the public eye, but the image of himself that he could glimpse there was not a unified one. He aroused admiration and contempt in equal measure, every plaudit was cancelled out by a brickbat. When he looked into this mirror, he must have seen his image fragmented into a thousand pieces. Like all artists, perhaps, Sartre was in search of his own face. This had been true since the child Poulou had discovered that language was a mirror – as well as being a window onto the world. The celebrity that was about to burst upon Sartre merely served to underline his dilemma.

Two weeks after *Huis clos* opened, the allies landed in Normandy; two months later they were in Paris. The occupation was at an end and the 'Sartre years' were about to begin.

3

The Price of Fame

The failure of 'Socialisme et Liberté' had given rise to a burst of creativity: two novels, two plays, five screenplays, eleven literary-critical articles and a seminal philosophical treatise. Apart from the sheer productivity, what is striking here is the variety of the work. Although Sartre was always, most fundamentally, a *writer*, it was philosophy that provided him with a technique and a methodology – a style of reasoning and a mode of exposition. From this base, Sartre colonized adjacent fields: the novel, theatre, cinema. In 1944 he was provided with the opportunity to extend his influence into the sphere of journalism. As the Allies advanced on Paris and liberation seemed only days away, Camus invited Sartre to write a series of eyewitness accounts of the events as they unfolded. Crisscrossing Paris on foot and on a bicycle in the last week of August 1944, Sartre witnessed the insurrection first-hand: the skirmishes and street-fighting as die-hard resistance was overcome by the Forces Françaises de l'Intérieur and by ordinary Parisians armed with whatever weapons they could lay their hands on; the joy of liberation, the relief and the triumph, but also the ugliness of triumphalism and reprisals: the summary beatings, the executions and the humiliation of collaborators. The purges had begun. Debates in the CNE were increasingly dominated by questions of revenge and by the settling of scores: which writers and journalists had collaborated the most? What punishment would be fitting? If rank and file members of the French gestapo deserved to die, what about writers

March of the Comité du Front National du Spectacle, in memory of the victims of the Nazis, Paris, 16 October 1944. Sartre is immediately below the word *THEATRE*.

such as Brasillach or Céline (who had written rabidly anti-Semitic pamphlets)? A thornier question was that of the publishers: after all, somebody had to publish the future work of this committee of writers. In the event, publishers emerged relatively unscathed from the purges of the liberation (although Denoël, it is true, was gunned down in the street in 1945); Sartre's publisher, Gaston Gallimard, pleaded that he had continued to publish work by anti-Nazi writers; he also made an interesting proposal to Sartre: Gallimard would finance a new review with Sartre as its director. As the purges gathered pace all over France, and the bickering within the CNE continued through autumn 1944, Sartre spent less and less time at CNE meetings – increasingly dominated by the Communists – instead devoting his energies to putting together the editorial team of his new plaything.

In December 1944 Camus came to Sartre with another proposal: a delegation of French journalists was to make an official visit to the USA and Camus wanted Sartre to join them as the representative of his newspaper *Combat*.

When Sartre flew out in January 1945, aged 39, it was the first time that he had been outside of Europe. A photograph taken on the airport tarmac at San Antonio shows Sartre dwarfed by his fellow journalists, looking rather detached in the background – a stance he would adopt throughout the five-month trip. He had long 'known' America, through the *Nick Carter* and *Buffalo Bill* comics of his childhood, through the writers he regarded as the *avant-garde*: Faulkner, Hemingway, Dos Passos, and above all through jazz and through the cinema. But this was the real thing: endless travelling from aircraft factory to tank factory, from power-station to hydro-electric project. The dreary whirl of dreary receptions. An audience at the White House, concerts at Carnegie Hall. The fact that Sartre understood very little English, and spoke even less, could not have helped his immersion in this 'official' culture. He was more at home with the *émigré* artists, writers, filmmakers and intellectuals who had formed a loose colony in New York: Adorno, Brecht, Marcuse, Lévi-Strauss, the surrealists Tanguy and Masson. Even so, given what is known about his aversion for

Sartre and French journalists visit General George C. Marshall at his office in the Pentagon. Marshall is seated to the far left, Sartre is standing second from the left.

intellectual chit-chat, one suspects that his meeting with Charlie Parker and the evenings he spent soaking up the jazz at Nick's Bar were more to his liking.

For all that, the articles he sent back were, for the most part, flat, uninspired and uninspiring. This is partly explained by his lack of enthusiasm for military hardware and feats of civil engineering, but it is probably also related to the language itself: Sartre needed to be in France – even better, in Paris itself – in order to be *in* his language: in later life he often commented on his intensely proprietorial relationship to the French language.[1]

Two encounters of lasting importance took place outside of the official circus. The first was personal. A chance encounter with a compatriot, Dolorès Vanetti, was the start of the only relationship that would challenge the stability of the duo he formed with Beauvoir. The latter admitted in 1974 that Dolorès was 'the only one who had [her] worried'. For the remainder of his stay, Dolorès put her English at the service of Sartre and, as he later said, 'gave America to [him]'.[2]

The second encounter was even more important. At the end of the State Department-sponsored schedule of trips and events, the journalists were let loose to explore on their own. Sartre took himself off to Texas and New Mexico. It was there that he encountered poverty, racism and grinding oppression. The seven articles that arose out of that trip were imbued with a feeling that was quite lacking in the anodyne reports he had filed from the official circuit. He remarks in an article published in July 1945 that 'the black problem is neither political nor cultural: the Blacks belong to the American proletariat and their cause is the same as that of the white workers.'[3] A few years later, he would modify this pseudo-Marxist view – notably in 'Orphée noir', where he recognizes that anti-black racism has a specificity that sets it apart from the oppression suffered by the white proletariat. Above all, this encounter with the Otherness of Deep South racism induced Sartre to reflect on French colonial racism. This reveals something important about the way he functioned intellectually. Recognition of the self necessarily passes through recognition of the Other. What Sartre observed 'over there' in the USA opens up reflection on what is happening 'back here' – in France and its colonies. In a quite different context, and to different effect, this same dialectic would preside over the self-analysis that Sartre conducted through his biographies of certain chosen others: Baudelaire, Mallarmé, Genet, Flaubert etc. Reflexivity and *auto-critique* were to become the guiding principles of *Les Temps modernes* – the new review that started appearing in October 1945 – and anti-colonialism would be its most consistent editorial line.

The commencement of the new academic year in September (known in French as *la rentrée*) is the most important date in the French literary calendar. There could have been few *rentrées* as momentous as that of 1945, and none where one man had so completely dominated the front pages.

In September 1945, the first two volumes of Sartre's novel trilogy were published simultaneously. *L'Age de raison* had been completed as early as 1941, upon his return from the Stalag; the second volume – *Le Sursis* – was written in the flurry of activity of 1943–44. Given that the first volume was set in June 1938, and the second volume in September of that year (at the moment of the 'Munich crisis') there was already a considerable gap between the actuality of the novels' action and the actuality of the reader of 1945. Correspondingly, the problems preoccupying its protagonist had, apparently, long since been resolved by its author. In the literary-critical essays he published from 1938, Sartre had talked about matching, as far as possible, the temporality of the novel's action with that of the reader; he certainly adhered to that prescription in *L'Age de raison*, the action of which takes place in just two days. Mathieu Delarue – a thirty-something philosophy teacher – has many of the traits of the Sartre of the mid-late 1930s: for want of a positive reason to commit himself, he avoids commitments of all kinds; he interprets freedom in terms of the avoidance of any constraint or obligation. The crisis erupts when his long-term lover Marcelle announces that she is pregnant. The action of the novel, such as it is, consists of Mathieu's efforts to procure the money for an abortion which, unbeknownst to him, Marcelle no longer even wants. At the end of the two days, Mathieu has split with Marcelle, been rejected by Ivich (a young student he had been timidly pursuing), and has himself rejected the overtures of his friend Brunet to join the Communist party and give meaning to his life through collective struggle. He has retained his freedom, but to what end? Freedom is not an object that one can simply keep in a safe place until one is ready to use it. As he sits alone contemplating the ruins of his life, he is forced to admit that his precious freedom is no more than a worthless abstraction: 'For nothing: this life was given to him for nothing, he was nothing and yet he would never change: he was finished.'[4]

It was the negativity of this conclusion that inspired Sartre to publish the first two volumes together, for, in the overall scheme of the trilogy, Mathieu would indeed change – in precisely the way that Sartre himself thought he had changed since before the war: Mathieu, too, would discover his historicity, his *de facto* solidarity with other men, and perhaps even a positive commitment.

The individual drama of *L'Age de raison* becomes a collective drama in *Le Sursis*. In retrospect, Sartre identified the Munich crisis as the moment when he himself understood that he was not a self-contained monad, but was, like everyone else, open and permeable to the forces of historical change. In *Le Sursis*, he attempted to present the impending war as a reality that was simultaneously everywhere and nowhere: the fabric of everyone's existence, the context of everyone's thoughts, the background to everyone's actions, yet still elusive and impalpable. In order to achieve this, he had recourse to a formal innovation for which nothing could have prepared readers of his previous works. Borrowing from the 'simultaneist' technique of Dos Passos, he tried to show each moment of the Munich crisis as it was experienced simultaneously all over Europe, and beyond, by individuals directly affected by it, or, interestingly, who were completely oblivious to it. The small constellation of characters gravitating around the central figure of Mathieu now became a cast of thousands; well, about a hundred in fact. If, as the philosopher Pascal said of the universe, the war was an infinite sphere whose centre is everywhere but whose circumference is nowhere, then the intention was to multiply the centres, or individual consciousnesses, to such an extent that an impression of totality was created. Despite the virtuosity with which Sartre shifts the narrative point of view from character to character – sometimes quite seamlessly within a single sentence – the attempt was obviously destined to fail: had he created a thousand or even a million characters, the total picture would have eluded representation. What is more, the linearity of the literary medium (one word must follow another), no matter how slick the transitions, means that a text can never do more than approximate to simultaneity. Hailed as a bold failure by contemporary critics, *Le Sursis* is regarded today as one of Sartre's finest literary achievements. Most critics looked forward to the third volume to see where these roads to freedom would lead the protagonist: in the event, they would have to wait four years, by which time it was no longer clear why the journey had been undertaken in the first place.

Hot on the heals of *L'Age de raison* and *Le Sursis* came the eagerly awaited first issue of Sartre's new journal – named *Les Temps modernes* (TM) after Chaplin's film *Modern Times*. The core of the editorial board was Sartre, Beauvoir, Aron and Merleau-Ponty: philosophers one and all, and friends since their days at the ENS. The board also included the writer and ethnographer Michel Leiris and the influential *éminence grise* of French letters, Jean Paulhan. For the first issue in October 1945 Sartre wrote a *Présentation* setting forth the editorial policy of the review. The text is a veritable manifesto of what was starting to be known as 'committed literature'. The themes were simple and few in number: the writer is responsible for what he writes or does not write; the writer must write for the present, not for some unknowable posterity. Some – like André Gide – affected to read it as an agenda for socialist realism, but the political line of the journal was actually sketched in terms so vague as to be virtually meaningless: 'We line up alongside those who want to change at one and the same time the social condition of man and the conception that he has of himself.'[5] The *Présentation* actually looked back to the recent dark past of France as much as it did to a brave new world. Talking about writers like Voltaire and Zola – who had taken a stance against injustice – Sartre writes: 'each of these writers, in one particular circumstance of his life, took stock of his responsibility as a writer. The occupation taught us our responsibility.'[6] If writers like Brasillach had considered themselves irresponsible, the counterproof had been delivered in the most dramatic fashion: Brasillach had been shot for collaboration in February 1945. In a phrase that incensed the bourgeois literary establishment, Sartre continued: 'I consider Flaubert and Goncourt to be responsible for the repression of the Paris Commune because they did not write a single line to prevent it.'[7] Sartre was also looking to the past when he insisted that writers should write for the present and not for posterity. To his own past, to be precise: as we saw, the myth of posthumous glory was the very 'misunderstanding' that led the child Sartre to be a writer in the first place. Even in *La Nausée*, Roquentin ultimately seeks 'salvation' in the eyes of an unknown future reader. Never had Sartre written against himself with more fervour and more glee!

The best indication of a political line comes when Sartre marks off *TM* both from the bourgeois 'spirit of analysis' (that sees no groups, only an aggregate of individuals) and the Marxist 'spirit of synthesis' (that sees no individuals, only collectives): 'As for us, we refuse to allow ourselves to be torn between the thesis and the antithesis. We have no difficultly in conceiving that a man, although totally conditioned by his situation, may remain an irreducible centre of indetermination.'[8] The detail of the argument may have eluded some readers but the new watchwords were clear enough: freedom, responsibility, commitment.

The problem was that commitment was fast becoming the monopoly of the PCF, which was busy extracting every last ounce of credibility from its dominant role in the wartime resistance.

The last of the seven articles Sartre wrote for *Combat* concludes with these words: 'Tomorrow will be a very gloomy Sunday, an empty Sunday; the morning after the night before. And, on Monday, the shops and the offices will reopen: Paris will get back to work.'[9] He was right: once the euphoria of liberation had faded, the Communists, in particular, got back to work. That work included attacking Sartre, whom they cast as the high priest of a 'philosophy of despair'. The Communist weekly *Action* published a stream of articles attacking Sartre's 'pessimism' and accusing him of 'demoralizing our youth'. In December 1944, just before his departure for the USA, Sartre exercised his right of reply and published a short piece in *Esprit* in order to 'set the record straight'. Accepting for the first time the label 'Existentialist' – used as an insult by the Communists – he took the charges one by one and tried to demonstrate that Existentialism was a 'humanist philosophy of action, of effort, of struggle and of solidarity'. Clearly, the Communists were not convinced, for a year on the attacks had, if anything, increased in virulence. Thus it was that in October 1945 Sartre accepted an invitation to give a public lecture entitled 'Existentialism is a Humanism' in an attempt to defend himself against this unrelenting attack. He was also coming under fire from the Catholic right, whose reproaches were, substantially, the same as those of the Communists.

But Sartre had other motives for delivering this lecture. Existentialism was suddenly on everyone's lips. People were discovering his earlier work, and in particular *L'Etre et le néant*. Everyone knew the title, but few had read it cover to cover. This was hardly surprising. *L'Etre et le néant* is a highly technical piece of writing, engaging with the thought of major thinkers from Descartes to Heidegger: how could a non-specialist public expect to follow the finer points of Sartre's disputation with Kant and Heidegger when most had never even heard of these thinkers, let alone read them? The language of the book was a stumbling block: quite apart from the normal philosophical jargon, the work contained confusing neologisms as well as Sartre's own idiosyncratic rendering of German terms. And yet the work included elements that could lead readers to believe they were following the plot: one of the novelties of Sartre's approach is the way he uses banal, everyday situations in order to illustrate the most abstruse points. Thus one finds almost novelistic descriptions of the exaggerated gestures of a café waiter; memorable vignettes, such as the one that illustrates 'bad faith' by the example of the young woman allowing herself to be seduced 'without realizing it'; dialogic confrontations such as that between the homosexual and the 'champion of sincerity'. The readability of the long section on 'Concrete Relations with Others' (love, desire etc.) is enhanced by compelling glosses on everyday expressions, such as 'to be everything in the world for somebody' or 'I only have eyes for you'. Then there are the slogans, the most notorious of which is 'man is a useless passion'. This somewhat poetic phrase is perfectly clear if one has read and understood the preceding 600 pages, but if one hasn't, it could mean anything and everything. And that was the problem: Sartre thought he had written a tightly argued treatise but now he found himself taken to task for things he had never written; the meaning of his work was starting to slip away from him and return in a travestied form. An important motive for giving this lecture was therefore the desire to regain control over the meaning of his own thought (in later years, notably in connection with the play

Les Mains sales, he would make other such attempts, before finally realising their futility).

The *Club Maintenant* lecture was the big event of the *rentrée* of 1945. One way of appreciating the hysteria surrounding the lecture is to read Boris Vian's burlesque transposition of it in his 1947 novel *L'Ecume des jours.* He has Jean-Sol Partre arriving at the hall in a howdah atop an elephant and departing in a helicopter amid scenes of mayhem and pandemonium.[10] The howdah and the helicopter were inventions, but the rest was scarcely exaggerated: demand for places far outstripped supply, and there were unseemly scenes – scuffles, fisticuffs, broken chairs, people fainting in the unseasonable heatwave. When he eventually spoke – without notes – he delivered a measured and concise summary of the 'highlights' of *L'Etre et le néant* which was also a point by point rebuttal of the criticisms of Communists and Catholics alike. He tried to draw some ethical conclusions from his ontology, thus adding to the repertoire of Sartrean slogans: 'man is nothing more than what he makes (of) himself'; 'man is responsible for what he is'; 'our responsibility extends to the whole of humanity' etc. Describing Existentialism as nothing more than 'an effort to explore all the consequences of a coherent atheism', he claims that it provides 'an ethics of action and commitment'. The words were clearly intended to be balm to the ears of the Communists, but, in fairness, it is not surprising that the latter remained unimpressed. In truth, Sartre's position remained individualistic and, to a large degree, idealistic. A gulf lay between the abstract solidarity expressed by the phrase 'in choosing (for) himself, the individual chooses (for) all men' and the concrete solidarity of real groups engaged in real struggles. The attempt to reconcile the *ontological* freedom of the individual with the *praxis* of groups would occupy Sartre for the rest of his life.

The fact that Existentialism was fast becoming a fashion accessory did nothing to help him win over his detractors: young men

and women, dressed entirely in black, only coming out at night –
and even then wearing dark glasses! – started calling themselves
'Existentialists' and frequenting the jazz cellars of Saint-Germain-
des-Prés on the Left Bank. Followers of this first post-liberation
fashion adopted what they took to be the lifestyles and ideas of
writers like Sartre, Beauvoir and Camus. The fact that Sartre was
more likely to be found at his mother's flat playing a four-handed
piano sonata was, of course, neither here nor there. And there
were, undeniably, some circumstantial connections between Sartre
and this bohemian lifestyle: a notorious scene in *L'Age de raison* –
albeit set in 1938 – took place in a *louche* jazz cellar; Sartre *was* a
friend of Boris Vian – jazz trumpeter, writer, polymath and 'prince
of Saint-Germain-des-Prés'; he *had* written a song for the *chanteuse*
Juliette Gréco, and he *was* a jazz lover himself, even if his tastes
were somewhat 'old hat'. He did not, fortunately, favour black polo-
necks and drainpipe trousers. In fact, the adoration he attracted as
the *maître à penser* (or 'intellectual guru') of a whole new generation
probably weighed more heavily on his shoulders than did the odium
heaped on him by his ideological opponents.

In his recent work on Sartre, Bernard-Henri Lévy devotes a
whole section to 'hatred'. The insults of the Communists tended
to be mechanical and formulaic: bourgeois lackey/hyena/running-
dog, petty bourgeois idealist, etc. The still active Pétainist right
deployed rather more imagination, the Catholic weekly *Samedi Soir*
being his main antagonist. The latter preferred similes based on
various forms of excrement to the zoological metaphors of the
Communists. One of them compared Sartre's philosophy to 'shit-
covered paths where one should venture only if wearing stilts.'[11]
The director of *Le Figaro* at least evinced concern for Sartre's
immortal soul: 'the time has come to exorcise him, to smear him
with sulphur and to set fire to him in front of Notre Dame – which
would be the most charitable way of saving his soul'. One could
conclude from Sartre's ability to annoy the Stalinist PCF and the

Catholic right in equal measure that he must have being doing something right.

The puppet-king Egisthe, in *Les Mouches*, laments: 'what am I save the fear that other people have of me?' Sartre, too, must have experienced the vertigo that accompanies the draining of the self and its replacement by the irreconcilable judgements of other people: 'It is not pleasant to be treated like a public monument when one is still alive.'[12] It was probably with some relief, then, that he took off for the USA in December 1945 for a protracted visit with Dolorès. His fame preceded him, but not the hatred. Treated like a veritable star, he gave public lectures at all of the Ivy League universities and even 'played' the Carnegie Hall.

The brouhaha had not died down when he returned to Paris in spring 1946: the text of 'Existentialism is a Humanism' had been published just before his return, and the controversies continued. As if trying to match the publicity of the previous *rentrée*, he chose autumn of that year for the premiere of two new plays. Each of them caused a furore, albeit for different reasons. On 8 November, *Morts sans sépulture* and *La Putain respectueuse* starting playing on an alternating bill at the Théâtre Antoine.

The first was a bleak play about torture: a group of *maquisards* are being tortured one by one by the *milice* (French gestapo) with a view to forcing them to betray their leader. The play's tension lies less in whether they will divulge the information than in their individual reactions to the ordeal, both before and after. The violence of the torture scenes, and that fact that one of the victims is raped, provoked a scandal. At a moment when erstwhile collaborators were already feeling bold enough to crawl out of the holes where they had been hiding (by 1950, several 'men of Vichy' would actually be back in government), the play touched a raw nerve in its depiction of the *milice*. In the light of Sartre's ongoing problems with the PCF, it is worth noting that the 'positive hero' of the play, if it has one, is a Greek Communist.

The second play dealt in a rather burlesque manner with the serious subject of anti-black racism – a subject that was in the news at the time due to a rash of recent lynchings in the USA. The central characters are a prostitute and a black who takes refuge in her home: he is being hunted by a lynching party for a sexual assault on a white woman that was actually committed by the leader of the lynch-mob himself – the son of a local senator. Having witnessed the incident, the prostitute initially resists the blandishments of the senator, who attempts to persuade her to change her testimony and see the truth 'differently', but is finally seduced by the illusion of a share in the 'American dream'. It was the title of the play, more than its subject matter and its perceived anti-Americanism, which provoked the biggest scandal. The word *putain* (whore) was considered unseemly and had to be replaced on posters by the letter P!

The major text of the *rentrée* was *Réflexions sur la question juive*. This is one of Sartre's most influential texts, though its influence dated more from its republication by Gallimard in 1954 than from its first edition with the little-known publisher Paul Morihien. This was an 'occasional piece' and one whose genesis it is difficult to reconstruct. Sartre had started work on it two years previously and numerous references suggest that it had benefited from his two visits to the USA, but in the absence of a manuscript, it is hard to say precisely when it was written. The thesis of the text is apparently clear: there is no 'Jewish problem', the problem lies with the anti-Semite. The Jew is he who is held to be a Jew by the Other. The most accomplished – and longest – section of the text is devoted to a portrait of the anti-Semite, but the most controversial chapters were those that dealt with the authentic and the inauthentic Jew. Having discussed and eliminated race and culture as determining characteristics of a Jewish 'essence', Sartre concludes that all that remains of this essence is the historical and social situation in which the Jew is designated as a Jew. In this context, the authentic Jew is he who takes on board and defiantly revindicates the situation that has been made for him; inauthenticity consists in denying this situation: 'Authenticity for [the Jew] is to live to the very end his condition as Jew, inauthenticity consists in denying it or in attempting to get around it.'[13] The inauthentic Jew will try to 'assimilate' and thus reject his condition. The failure of this kind of assimilation had been illustrated in grotesque fashion as recently as 1942–44 when French Jews who did not even know that they were Jews were deported to Auschwitz after being denounced by anti-Semitic neighbours. And yet, Sartre sees assimilation as the long-term answer to the 'Jewish question': to attempt assimilation while anti-Semitism still persists is inauthentic, but when anti-Semitism itself disappears, then so too, logically, will the Jew.

While few doubted Sartre's good will, many criticised the assumptions he made, as a gentile, about Jewishness. Jews in particular criticized him for his lack of historical perspective, but also for his failure to recognise that there existed a certain Jewish subjectivity which could not be reduced to the simple interiorization of an external judgement. The essay is an example of what would now be called 'applied Sartreanism'.

In these years after the liberation Sartre was constantly playing 'catch-up' with himself: every text or lecture in which he popularized, or vulgarized, his philosophy for a non-specialist public gave rise to attacks and criticisms from specialists; these in turn obliged him to redefine his position and correct the misapprehensions that had arisen. This was the case with the short text in *Esprit*, referred to above, and with 'Existentialism is a Humanism' – the latter provoking a distinctly sharp response from Heidegger himself in 1946. In the editorials he had written for the first two issues of *TM*, he had launched the term 'committed literature', but with relatively little explanation. Largely in response to the criticism of what some saw as an empty slogan, Sartre undertook a long explanatory essay that was published in *TM* in 1947 under the title *Qu'est-ce que la littérature?* This is one of the best known and least understood of his works. Broadly, it offers a critique of the traditional bourgeois conception of the role of the writer, and proposes a new model of the 'committed writer' who will write for his age. Sartre's personal evolution is, of course, encapsulated in these two figures. The work is divided into four chapters. It begins with a rather technical discussion of the question 'What is writing?' It will be recalled that, in *L'Imaginaire*, Sartre had divorced artistic creation of all kinds from the domain of ethics. Given the urgent, ethical imperative of *Qu'est-ce que la littérature?*, this was now something of an embarrassment. He resolves the problem by now declaring that there is at least one area of artistic endeavour that has a more or less direct relation to reality, and that is prose writing: 'The [prose] writer deals in significations. Let us be clear about this: the empire of signs is prose; poetry is on the side of painting, sculpture and music.'[14] The writer of prose uses language in a transitive, 'instrumental' way, in order to act on his readers and to act on the world. His words are transparent windows onto a world of shared reality. But the poet is like Narcissus: his words, in their opacity, are little more than mirrors in which he contemplates his own image. The idea that language is a practical tool was already present in *L'Etre et le néant*, where it is presented as an extension of the body itself; in *Qu'est-ce que la littérature?*, the overriding concern is to make writing what it *has to be*, if it is to concord with Sartre's new-found political and social militancy, namely, a form of action: to write is to act. And that is because, again in line with the analyses of *L'Etre et le néant*, to name an object is already to reveal or 'unveil' it to someone else, and in so doing to change it.

The next chapter ('Why does one write?') is in many ways the most interesting in what it reveals about Sartre's own choice of writing – suggesting that something of the narcissism of the poet persists even in the communicative attitude of the prose-writer. One writes, fundamentally, in order to feel essential in relation to one's creation; but since our constitutive contingency condemns us to inessentiality, this aim is destined to remain unfulfilled: there can be no justification for existing. Fortunately, the reader is there: in the next chapter ('For whom does one write?') we read that 'art only exists for and by the other'[15] and 'every literary work is an appeal' – an appeal from the writer who freely creates his work, to a reader who freely takes up this work and (re)creates it. Writing is an appeal, therefore, from one freedom to another, an act of non-coercive mutual recognition. Of course, the reader may simply put down the book and refuse to collaborate with the writer in this remaking of the world; this is why literary creation is also said by Sartre to be a moment of *risk* where the author puts himself in danger, outside in the world. If other people are crucial to the artist's endeavour, they are no longer the abstract 'others' (*autrui*) of *L'Etre et le néant*: they are the real men of flesh and blood who are the author's contemporaries. In a remarkable phrase – of albeit dubious agronomic accuracy – Sartre remarks: 'Apparently, bananas taste better when they are consumed on the spot: books also.' In other words, the writer should write for the here and now, not for some uncertain posterity.

But which 'here and now'? The long concluding chapter of the book ('Situation of the writer in 1947') relates how Sartre's own experience of captivity and of occupation had led him to realize that, like it or not, we are all implicated in the march of history: there is no 'outside' of history, there is no Olympus from which the writer may serenely survey the futile agitation of the mortals beneath him. Once the writer has grasped the meaning of this *de facto* commitment to his epoch, his task consists in elucidating the nature of that commitment, for himself and for his readers. In so doing, he must be aware that both he and his readers start from a position of mystification and alienation: 'Nazism was a mystification, Gaullism is another, Catholicism a third; it is now beyond doubt that French Communism is a fourth.'[16] In this ideo-logical configuration, the writer's job must be to demystify: 'We must reveal to the reader, in each specific instance, his power to do and to undo, in short, to act.'[17]

The major themes of *Qu'est-ce que la literature?* – alienation, commitment, generosity, creativity – occur repeatedly in other texts dating from this moment in 1947–48. He wrote, for example, some 600 pages of an Ethics (published posthumously as the *Cahiers pour une morale*) before abandoning it and dismissing it as 'an ethics by and for writers': the idealized relationship between writer and reader, engaged jointly in a struggle to overcome alienation, was not so easy to translate into the historical struggle between antagonistic classes.

More intriguing – given the way he had denigrated poetry as 'narcissistic' in *Qu'est-ce que la littérature?* – is the prevalence of poetry in texts of this period. In 1947 he was invited to write a preface for Léopold Senghor's *Anthologie de la nouvelle poésie nègre et malgache de langue française.* The superb text that he produced was entitled '*Orphée noir*'. In it he retracts, or at least nuances, some of the more dismissive remarks he had made about poetry in *Qu'est-ce que la littérature?* Indeed, he declares that 'black, French-language poetry is, today, the only great revolutionary poetry'.[18] The very qualities that had seemingly made poetry unfit for commitment – its closedness, its opacity – are now seen to endow it with a remarkable revolutionary and subversive potential. The poet is still a narcissist, but the black Narcissus succeeds in universalizing his self, such that his struggle (against colonial racism) becomes the struggle of all men against oppression. This text went a long way towards establishing Sartre's credentials amongst third-world intellectuals and freedom fighters.

An ethical concern is clearly present in *Baudelaire*, the first of Sartre's existential biographies, published in 1947. This was not Sartre's first attempt at the genre: the *Carnets de la drôle de guerre* contain many pages of analysis of Kaiser Wilhelm, using data gleaned from a conventional biography of the emperor by Karl

Ludwig. In a section of *L'Etre et le néant* entitled 'La Psychanalyse Existentielle', Sartre had sketched a method of biographical enquiry intended to be synthetic rather than analytic: whereas traditional biographies tend simply to juxtapose the discrete biographical data without integrating them, Sartre sought a method whereby the known data – as heterogeneous as it may appear – would be unified by the life project of the subject: what he called the 'original project'. Freudian psychoanalysis and Marxism are both synthetic in this sense, but each had different shortcomings, thought Sartre: psychoanalysis subordinates the data to pervasive unconscious forces; Marxism, on the other hand, simply discounts interiority by subsuming it under the 'objective' forces of historical determination. As early as this, Sartre was seeking a method that would somehow synthesize subjectivity and objectivity. There was a third important strand to Sartre's biographical impulse: the early sketch of Kaiser Wilhelm was conducted in the midst of an extensive self-portrait; Sartre's writing about others was also self-reflective. That is, the language and concepts he employed were both a window onto another person's life, and a mirror in which he hoped to catch a glimpse of himself. (We only ever glimpse ourselves *as another* in moments when we come upon our reflection unawares: when, for example, we round a corner and are confronted by our reflection in a shop-window that we had assumed to be transparent.) In this way, then, Sartre's existential biographies – if not explicitly autobiographical – are self-reflective.

Having said this, the study of Baudelaire is notable more for its ambition than for its achievements. In it, Sartre set out to demonstrate that Baudelaire was not the archetypal *poète maudit*, but that he had – like all of us – precisely the life he deserved. The original project of Baudelaire, says Sartre, was to be subjugated by the gaze of the Other. Once this choice has been posited, it serves as the unifying thread for the disparate data of Baudelaire's life: his dandyism, his spiritualism, his sexuality, his cult of artificiality, his horror of nature and, of course, his poems. Where the study is inadequate is in its failure to take sufficient account of the objective spirit of the age: any number of Baudelaire's contemporaries possessed these same traits. By the same token, the study perhaps misses the work carried out by the poet on these existing conditions: only he, unlike the mass of his contemporaries, transformed those givens into some of the greatest poetry of the nineteenth century. The technical mastery of poetic form tends to disappear, in Sartre's study, behind a vision of the poems as merely symptomatic.

Beauvoir remarks in her memoirs that the impetus behind the founding of *Les Temps modernes* had been 'to provide post-war France with an ideology', the implication being that the established parties and existing ideologies of left and right were already bankrupt. Since 1945 France had been governed by a 'liberation coalition' of Socialists (SFIO), Gaullists (MRP) and Communists. Once the euphoria of the liberation had worn off, the faultlines began to appear and the players quickly resorted to ideological type. By 1947, whatever fragile consensus there had been was crumbling fast. In January 1946 de Gaulle left the government when his attempts to enhance the power of the executive *vis-à-vis* parliament were rebuffed by the Socialists and the Communists. In May 1947 it was the turn of the Communists, who were excluded by the Socialist Ramadier because of their opposition to the Marshall Plan. This was the beginning of the Cold War. With sixteen European countries embracing the Marshall doctrine, and the Soviet Union and its satellites rejecting it, the world was fast polarizing around American imperialism, on the one hand, and Soviet Communism on the other. Sartre's preferred stance for Europe was one of critical neutrality – the politics of the third way ('troisième voie').

In *Qu'est-ce que la littérature?* Sartre had urged writers to embrace the emerging mass media in order to get their message across to the widest possible audience. In October 1947 he was provided with the opportunity to do just that when the Ramadier government was persuaded (by an old friend of Sartre's) to give *TM* a regular spot on State radio: a team from the review would discuss, every week, the burning questions of political actuality. The first programme in the series was broadcast live on 20 October 1947. The uproar was deafening: the participants had launched an intemperate attack on de Gaulle, likening him (via the metonymy of his moustache) to Pétain and Hitler! Despite the scandal, the programmes continued until November, at which time the government that had sanctioned them itself fell.

But as the doors of state radio closed, another one opened – this one leading to Sartre's first, and only, experiment in practical third-way politics. In the context of the rapidly degenerating international situation, Sartre had readily signed two 'Appeals to International Opinion' launched by a small group of left-wing journalists. The line was clear enough: a refusal to take sides in the nascent Cold War and a desire to create an independent, socialist Europe, as a 'third way'. Two of the instigators of the Appeal, Georges Altman and David Rousset, contacted Sartre to ask him to join a new political movement that would actively pursue this 'third way'. He accepted and took up joint leadership of the movement from 1947. The *Rassemblement Démocratique Révolutionnaire* (RDR) was, as its name suggests, not a political party but a gathering, a movement of all those on the Left who were disaffected with the response of the established parties (principally the Communists and the Socialists) to the international crisis: in theory, it was possible to 'adhere' to the RDR whilst remaining a member of another party. Much has been written about the RDR and Sartre's involvement in it – perhaps more than it deserves, for, by the time it imploded in 1949, it had a mere 2,000 paid-up members. This was Sartre's one and only experience of 'practical' political organization, and it was not a happy one. His progressive disaffection with the RDR was due in large part to his suspicion that his co-leaders were being inexorably sucked into the American sphere of influence

– not least at the level of finance. He was probably correct, but, for all that, one is struck by the extent to which criticisms of his lukewarm engagement in the practical work of the RDR resemble those made of his inaptitude for practical action at the time of *Socialisme et Liberté*. David Rousset later remarked: 'He had the keenest interest in the play and the movement of ideas, but he had relatively little curiosity about events and did not have a passionate interest in the world . . . Yes, that was it, basically Sartre lived in a bubble.'[19]

Sartre left the RDR less with a bang than with a whimper, preferring to become gradually invisible. Just before the 1949 summer congress of the RDR he had departed France to visit Central America and the Caribbean with Dolorès. For a second time, the gulf between intellectual speculation and concrete militancy had opened up under his feet.

It is an analogous opposition (between idealism and realism) that lies at the heart of *Les Mains sales* – a play that nevertheless dates from the honeymoon days of Sartre's involvement in the RDR in early 1948.

Les Mains sales is Sartre's most enduringly successful play. Its complex structure – employing a central flashback and numerous dramatic reversals – makes it difficult to summarize in a linear fashion. Set in a fictional Eastern European state towards the end of World War II, it centres on Hugo, a young bourgeois intellectual who has left his class to join the 'Proletarian Party'. Impatient with the pseudo-action of writing for the party newspaper, he demands to be entrusted with 'direct action'. He is given the job of winning the confidence of, and then assassinating, a party leader (Hoederer) who intends to draw the party into a politically pragmatic alliance with the Fascist Regent (who rules the country) and the social democratic opposition party (who are the strongest and best-armed faction of the resistance movement). Both Hoederer and the comrades who order his assassination are operating in the dark, as lines of communication with Moscow are broken: they must therefore 'invent'. The relationship between Hugo and the man he has been sent to kill is developed in the long central flashback. Despite two arguments in which Hugo's rather naïve idealism is opposed to the hard-headed pragmatism of Hoederer, Hugo finds himself drawn to the older man, perhaps as a positive substitute for his own despised father. Like Hamlet, he tergiversates and may well be on the point of renouncing his murderous plan, but at that moment chance intervenes: Hugo enters Hoederer's office unannounced to find his wife, Jessica, in the arms of the older man. He pulls the trigger. The end of the play returns to the present in which it began. Just released from jail where he had served a short sentence for committing this 'crime of passion', Hugo is now holed up in the house of a former lover, and Party member, Olga; outside are the Party's hitmen who have been ordered to 'liquidate' him. Olga has demanded that Hugo recount the circumstances of Hoederer's killing in order that she may judge whether he is 'recyclable' by the Party or not. But the meaning of his act now escapes him. How can he disentangle the political from the personal? Did he kill out of jealousy or because Hoederer was a traitor to the Party and its ideals? Now comes the *coup de théâtre* around which the whole play is built: whilst Hugo was in prison, communications have been re-established with Moscow and the orders from on high are to pursue precisely the politics of pragmatic compromise that Hoederer had attempted. So now his death, and his assassin, have become an embarrassment: the only 'acceptable' version of history is that his death was the result of a crime of passion. Upon hearing this, Hugo refuses to allow the meaning of his act to be determined by the lie-machine of the Party, and – believing that he is defining the death of Hoederer once and for all as a political assassination – he opens the door and throws himself in front of the assassins' bullets. He is wrong, of course: history is written by the victors, and, with Hugo out of the way, the Party will invent the version of Hoederer's death that it pleases.

This brief summary does no more than skim the surface of what is actually a complex and ambiguous play. In fact, no one in the play is wholly right or wrong: Hugo and Hoederer are each right and wrong at different moments. If Hoederer's commitment to the Cause was so unshakeable, then to jeopardize his work – and the lives he claims depend on it – for the sake of fleeting sexual gratification is unconscionably irresponsible; Hugo, on the other hand, saves nothing and nobody by his effective suicide: the meaning of his act is taken out of his hands forever. The debate around the status of truth and lies in the context of revolutionary action is also left without resolution.

But the struggle over meaning continued outside of the theatre: after a moment's hesitation, the bourgeois press greeted the play enthusiastically, which was enough to prompt the PCF and its press organs to denounce it as 'anti-Communist'. Despite his less than warm feelings towards the PCF (who were still engaged in their own Stalinist rewriting of the meaning of Sartre's friend Paul Nizan's life), Sartre refused to allow the play to be used an anti-Communist weapon. He later banned all future stagings – unless they had the explicit blessing of the Communist party of the country concerned. All of which brought home to Sartre the truth of the adage 'when a man throws a stick, who can tell where it will land?', or, as he put in the *Cahiers pour une morale*, 'the dimension of the future is ignorance, risk, uncertainty and gamble'.[20]

The third volume of *Les Chemins de la liberté*, published in 1949, was greeted with much less public and critical acclaim than had been the first two volumes four years earlier, and this despite the fact that it is arguably the most accomplished of the three volumes. Centred for the most part, still, on Mathieu Delarue, it recounts the debacle of May–June 1940. In fact, the planned trilogy had now expanded into a tetralogy; the fourth volume was to tell of Mathieu's imprisonment in a Stalag, his escape and his eventual death, under Gestapo torture, as a resistance fighter. Only fragments were ever written, and the novel cycle was to remain, like so many of Sartre's projects, unfinished. There could be many reasons for this, but the simplest is that Sartre probably did not know how to represent the 'free commitment' that was to lie at the end of these 'roads to freedom'. In the Manichaean context of the war against Nazism, good and bad were as clear as black and white; in the Europe of 1949 – and in the aftermath of the failure of the RDR – everything was an unhealthy shade of grey.

The decade that had seen Sartre rise from relative obscurity to literary stardom ended with him in a limbo. When the Korean War broke out in 1950 – raising the temperature of the Cold War by several degrees – Sartre found himself in a political and philosophical no-man's-land. Salvation, as we will see, was to arrive in the unlikeliest of forms.

4

The Shock of the Real

The collapse of the RDR was a public failure but it was accompanied by a failure of a different order that was quite invisible to his contemporaries. In 1947–48 he had written hundreds of pages of an Ethics that was to be the continuation of *L'Etre et le néant*. The problem was how to pass from the ontological freedom defined in that work to a free commitment to collective action. Although his intellectual armoury had been strengthened by his absorption of Alexandre Kojève's influential *Introduction à la lecture de Hegel*, he clearly felt that he lacked the 'tools' to go further; or rather that the tools he did possess condemned him to writing nothing more than 'an ethics by a writer for other writers'. So, in 1949–50 he wrote virtually nothing, instead starting to immerse himself in further study: history – especially that of nineteenth-century France – economics, a rereading of Marx. Indeed, in terms of *visible* literary production at least, the decade between 1949 and 1959 was a relatively lean period: four plays, of which one was an adaptation, and the complete abandonment of the novel form. The bulk of his publications in this period – with the notable exception of the voluminous preface to the *Œuvres complètes de Jean Genet* in 1952 – were political. Although he never dictated the editorial policy of *TM*, the contents pages of that review closely mirror the vagaries of Sartre's own preoccupations: the balance between articles devoted to literature and those devoted, broadly, to politics swings steadily in favour of the latter, such that,

between October 1945 and February 1951 literature stood at
35 per cent and politics at 26 per cent, whereas by 1963 that
proportion was reversed.[1]

The failure of the RDR affected Sartre more than one might
expect, given the brevity of the experiment. Beauvoir quotes from
Sartre's unpublished notes: 'The break-up of the RDR. A blow.
A new and definitive education in realism. One does not *create* a
movement.'[2] In order to understand this, one first has to understand what the RDR had represented for Sartre in terms of
personal opportunity. Above all, it represented the possibility of
resolving his own contradictions. The first of these involved his
uncomfortable position 'with one foot in the camp of the bourgeoisie and one foot in that of the proletariat'. He was born a
bourgeois and he exercised the most bourgeois of professions, but
he had renounced that class and all of its works: having decided
that the only ethical stance was to be unconditionally on the side of
the oppressed, and having identified the workers as the victims of
capitalist oppression, he *must* be with the masses. But the masses –
insofar as they were represented by the PCF – did not want to be
with him. The hostility of the PCF produced a second contradiction
– an existential variant of the first. As Beauvoir remarks, the
hatred of which Sartre was the object made it increasingly difficult
for him to maintain a 'good conscience': 'the hatred of others
reveals to me my objectivity',[3] meaning that he is unable to take
refuge from this *outside* judgement in the *subjective* certainty of
his solidarity with the workers. Effectively, he found himself in
the schizophrenic position of the individual whose every private
thought is accompanied by the anxiety: 'what would x say if
he knew?' But who was 'x'? Not so much the masses as the
ideologues of the PCF. Intriguingly, Sartre remarks: 'From 1947,
I had a double point of reference: I judged my principles also
on the basis of the principles of others – those of Marxism.'[4]
The PCF – to the extent that he was able to convince himself that

it was the concrete expression of living Marxism – had become Sartre's superego. In light of this, one could see the in-depth study that Sartre undertook of history, economy and Marx's writings less as an attempt to harmonize conflicting principles than as an attempt to learn, as it were, how his new 'superego' worked – the better to defuse its powers. After all, the culmination of this decade of research was a work which demonstrated that the PCF was the moribund embodiment of a dead, sclerotic Marxism: if the latter was to be brought back to life, it would need a bracing injection of negativity, subjectivity and transcendence: the very principles of . . . Sartrean Existentialism. Briefly, then, the RDR had represented an opportunity for Sartre to resolve his contradictions through collective political action, an attempt to rejoin the masses whilst avoiding the straitjacket of party membership.

The figure of the 'monster' starts to appear in Sartre's work in about 1947. In 'Orphée noir' the term is applied to the *compradores* – those strange, hybrid, partially assimilated intermediaries between their brothers in oppression and the colonizers whom they serve. It is also used to describe the situation of black Francophone writers who are similarly caught between the vernacular (that no one reads, often because it has no written form) and the language of the colonial oppressor. There is no doubt that Sartre had in mind a monster such as the minotaur or the centaur in which the man appears to have been frozen in mid-emergence from the beast. But he uses the term also for its etymology: *monstrare* in Latin means to show or display. The monster is a monster because of the disparity between his subjectivity and the way he is objectively constituted by the gaze of the other. This metaphor will become very active in Sartre's thought over the next fifteen years, providing him with a point of entry into a range of disparate lives. It is only in the mid-1960s that he realizes that monstrosity is simply descriptive of the human condition.

But we are back in 1950 now, and Sartre has at least eliminated one of the contradictions in his life: in June he ended his five-year relationship with Dolorès Vanetti, despite, or perhaps because of, the fact that she had now moved back to France. Elsewhere, relations with the Communists had reached a new low. Sartre's adherence to the RDR had prompted renewed personal attacks. The publication in 1949 of Beauvoir's *Le Deuxième Sexe* – the seminal work of modern feminism – had received a hostile press, predictably, from the Catholic bourgeois right, but also, more surprisingly, from the Communists. Sartre's erstwhile student Jean Kanapa, now a PCF hack, had seemingly been promoted to tormentor-in-chief. 'Things could not get any worse', wrote Beauvoir in her memoirs. But they could, and they did. Non-Communist left-wing intellectuals found themselves in a classic double-bind: 'Between the two blocs there was definitively no third way. And to choose between them was still impossible.'[5] The USA appeared to be intent on propping up every repressive regime in the world; only five years after the defeat of Fascism in Europe, the State Department now gave financial backing to Franco's Fascist dictatorship on France's southern border. It was against this dismal backdrop that the news of the Soviet labour camps broke. In fact, the existence of the 'corrective labour camps' and of 'administrative detention' (i.e. arbitrary arrest and imprisonment) had been in the public domain since 1936, but had been conveniently 'forgotten' as long as Nazism posed the greater threat. But now the 'Soviet Code of Corrective Labour' had been republished in England and openly discussed in the UN. It was still not, however, public knowledge in France. Sartre decided to publish the Code in *TM*, but the right-wing press beat him to it and mounted an enormous anti-Soviet campaign. As if the *facts* of the camps were not enough, newspapers published photographs of what purported to be Soviet 'death trains' that turned out to be doctored photographs of Nazi cattle-trucks bound for Auschwitz. Nonetheless, in January 1951, *TM* published the documents with an editorial by Sartre and Merleau-Ponty: 'There is no Socialism when one in twenty citizens is in a camp.' Not surprisingly, this did little to defuse the hostility of the PCF.

One text in particular from 1950 encapsulates Sartre's dilemmas and contradictions: his preface to Roger Stéphane's *Portrait de l'aventurier*. For Stéphane, as glossed by Sartre, the adventurer is essentially the bourgeois individualist, isolated from his fellows and, especially, from the masses: 'If the Ego comes first, one is separated for ever. In the bourgeoisie, the ego is born at a very early age . . . To be oneself is first and foremost not to be like one's neighbour; to be a "one-off" . . . Bourgeois civilization is a "*civilization of solitude*".[6] The adventurer may join a party or put his talents at the service of a liberation movement (the book discusses T. E. Lawrence amongst others), but his commitment, while total, will only ever be a gesture. The militant (or the 'average Communist'), on the other hand, is driven into the Party by hunger, fear or anger: his commitment is unreflecting. He knows no solitude as he moves in the masses and the masses move in him: 'He is constituted in his own eyes by rigorously objective facts, he is explained by his class, by the historical conjuncture; he sees himself from inside as he is seen from the outside: there are no secret dramas or hidden compartments.[7] The action of the militant is unimportant in itself: it is simply the means to achieve an end; but the end is irrelevant to the adventurer, it is merely the pretext for the means (action).

The opposition between Hugo and the Party militants in *Les Mains sales* is clearly readable in this diptych. Sartre repeatedly told interviewers that his own sympathies lay with the militants in that play, rather than with the bourgeois 'adventurer'. In light of this, the conclusion to his preface is unexpected. Having extolled the seeming 'authenticity' of the militant throughout, Sartre concludes: 'And yet, after having applauded the victory of

the militant, it is the adventurer that I will follow in his solitude',[8] and this because the adventurer has wrestled with the fundamental paradox of the human condition: 'man *exists* because he *is* impossible.'[9] The discipline of the militant needs to be 'humanized': 'Of course I know that any action is double-sided: negativity . . . and construction. We must restore negativity, restlessness [*inquiétude*] and reflexive self-criticism to discipline.'[10]

Sartre concocts a rhetorical solution to the problem of action in this preface, but the real dilemma was more than simply a form of words: 'The contradiction was not in the ideas. It was in my being. For this freedom that I *was* implied the freedom of all. And yet all were not free. I could not, without breaking under the strain, submit myself to the discipline of all. And I could not be free all by myself.'[11] It is precisely this impasse that lies at the heart of Sartre's next play, *Le Diable et le bon Dieu*, first performed in June 1951.

The play was well attended but it was not an unmitigated critical success, despite the towering central performance of Pierre Brasseur. It was deemed verbose and, at nearly four hours, it certainly strained the attention span of the audience. The end of the play was still unwritten when rehearsals commenced; the producer, Simone Berriau, viewed with dismay the arrival of each thick, hand-written scene: Sartre claimed that she strode round the theatre making unconscious scissor-movements with her fingers! For all that, the play is now regarded as one of Sartre's greatest theatrical achievements. It is set in the sixteenth-century Germany of the Peasants' Revolt and its dialogue is richly infused with the language of the philosophico-theological debates of the age (provoking, once again, the wrath of the Catholic establishment). But its real subject could not have been closer to Sartre's heart in 1951. Following on from *Les Mains sales* and the preface to Stéphane's book, he returns to the couple of the militant and the adventurer.

The hero (Goetz) thirsts for the absolute. He tries first to satisfy this thirst by doing Evil. When it is pointed out to him that doing evil is hardly a major achievement in an age where atrocity has become the norm, he abruptly 'converts' to Good, gives away his lands, disbands his armies and founds a sixteenth-century equivalent of a hippy commune governed by peace, love and equality. But whether he *tries* to do Good or Evil, the result remains the same: his actions serve only to reinforce the already powerful and to enrich the already rich. The key moment in the play is not the set-piece in which he realizes that the sky is empty and that man is alone and free (Oreste had already got that far in 1943), but the moment when he realizes that Nasty (the figure of the 'militant' in the play) is just as alone as he is. In accepting the command of the peasant forces in what he knows is a lost cause, Goetz fuses the existential solitude and critical negativity of the adventurer with the unshakeable faith of the militant. In a much misunderstood climactic moment, he instigates the 'reign of man' by the cold-blooded killing of a captain who refuses to serve under him. Goetz's final lines are quintessential Sartrean melodrama: 'Don't be afraid', he says to Nasty:

I will not weaken. I will make the men loathe me because I have no other way of loving them, I will give them orders because I have no other way of obeying, I will remain alone with the empty sky above me, because I have no other way of being with everyone. There is a war to be waged – and I will wage it.[12]

One of the notable themes of the play is the way that every action undertaken by its protagonist rebounds on him, producing the opposite effect to the one intended. Already in *Les Mains sales* the meaning of Hugo's action was stolen from him by others, but here Sartre goes one step further. We are a long way from the optimism of the occupation and the liberation, when Sartre believed

that *any* situation could be transcended and ultimately transformed by the sheer force of will of the authentic individual.
Beauvoir sums up this distance quite succinctly: 'In 1944 he
thought that any situation could be transcended by a subjective
movement: now, in 1951, he knew that circumstances sometimes
rob us of our transcendence; against them, no individual salvation
is possible, only a collective struggle.'[13]

No doubt, Sartre's successive 'lessons in realism' had been
instrumental in bringing him to this realization; but at the end
of *Le Diable et le bon Dieu*, the sword with which Pierre Brasseur
runs through the recalcitrant captain has a retractable blade; in
life, it is real steel cutting through real flesh. Sartre, this time,
produced an aesthetic solution to the problem of practical commitment. This fact hardly escaped him: in an interview, he made the
much-quoted remark 'I had Goetz do what I myself could not.'[14]
The imaginary is a place where all contradictions can be resolved.
But reality is a less comfortable place to inhabit. Before leaving
this play, it is worth noting a further appearance of the figure of
the monster. This time the monster takes the form of the 'bastard',
but the essential traits (hybridity, alienation, self-loathing) are all
present and clearly legible in an exchange between Goetz and
another 'bastard', Heinrich: 'Of course bastards betray: what do
you expect them to do? Me, I'm a double-agent from birth: my
mother gave herself to a peasant and I'm made of two halves that
don't stick together.'[15]

Bastardy and betrayal were also prominent themes in what was
without doubt Sartre's major work of the 1950s. Sartre had met
Jean Genet shortly before the liberation of Paris and had, along
with Jean Cocteau and others, been instrumental in securing a
provisional presidential pardon for Genet, who was facing life-
imprisonment for recidivism. Sartre's admiration for Genet and
familiarity with his work had led Gallimard to suggest that he
write a preface for that publisher's projected edition of Genet's

Complete Works. When it was finally published (as volume I of the *Œuvres Complètes de Jean Genet*), the preface ran to 578 pages! It is an infinitely more complex work than the previous study of Baudelaire, but the aim remains similar: 'To show the limits of psychoanalytic interpretation and of Marxist explanation, and to demonstrate that freedom alone can account for a person in his totality, to show this freedom at grips with destiny.'[16] According to Sartre, Genet's freedom was primordially alienated by an act of verbal violence committed on him when he was only a child and unable to relativize the crushing judgement of the collectivity. Caught pilfering from his adoptive family, Genet is transfixed by a 'vertiginous word': thief! The word is both act and gaze: 'Sexually, Genet is first and foremost a raped child. This first rape was the gaze of the Other that surprised him, penetrated him, transformed him forever into an object.'[17] Genet's existence is henceforth the attempt to *be* the object that others had made of him. Whilst this may sound like bad faith, Sartre is in fact describing a lifelong process of de-alienation whereby Genet recaptures his alienated freedom and turns it back onto those who had mutilated him. For *Saint Genet, comédien et martyr* is also a virulent critique of the bourgeois – the *Justes*, the *gens de bien* – who had used the child as a scapegoat: the Evil that was in them was exorcized and located *outside*, in this marginal figure. Sartre remarks that they had taken a child and turned him into a fairground geek (*monstre*) for reasons of social utility. Genet's liberation takes the form of a kind of counter-exorcism or catharsis – through writing – wherein the original possession is reversed and the bourgeois readers find themselves infected with their own negativity.

The very scope of Sartre's study disorientated its first readers: it blurred the boundaries between literary criticism, philosophy, psychoanalysis, sociology and anthropology in a way that was quite new at the time. In this respect, his subject was well chosen: Genet was marginal in every sense of the term (a thief, a homosexual, a poet . . .) and Sartre's analysis resonates sympathetically with contemporary anthropological thought on the importance of marginality in the construction of social cohesion.

In an interview that appeared on the very day of the premiere of *Le Diable et le bon Dieu*, Sartre opined: 'For the time being, the Communist party represents the proletariat as far as I am concerned, and I don't see that changing in the near future.'[18] But it was not only access to the French working class that was controlled by the PCF: the previous year, Sartre and Beauvoir had travelled to North and sub-Saharan Africa and attempted to make contact with the militants of Révolution Démocratique Africaine (RDA), but they were rebuffed by the African revolutionaries who had been informed by the PCF that Sartre and Beauvoir were traitors and spies! Despite this, the first moves towards a *rapprochement* came from the Communists. At the end of 1951 representatives of the PCF appealed to Sartre for help in the so-called Henri Martin affair. Henri Martin was an ensign in the French navy; he was also a Communist. He had been court-martialled and sentenced to five years in prison for protesting against French involvement in Indo-China (the very beginnings of what would turn into the Vietnam War). The PCF had launched a campaign to have him freed. Sartre agreed to support the campaign, and tensions between him and the Communists began to lessen. Later in 1952 Sartre moved even closer to his antagonists. In the spring of that year he was vacationing in Italy and following in the press the revelations about the increasingly dirty war in Korea. He learnt also that the PCF had organized a mass demonstration against the visit to Paris of the US general Ridgway who commanded the US forces in Korea. The police banned the demonstration but it went ahead anyway and resulted in violent street battles between protesters and police. On the evening of the demonstration, the acting secretary of the PCF, Jacques Duclos, was driving home with his wife when he was stopped by police.

They discovered what they claimed were carrier pigeons in the boot of his car. The birds – actually destined for Duclos's pot – were obviously proof of a plot against the state: Duclos was arrested and would eventually spend a year in jail. When Sartre read about this he curtailed his vacation and immediately returned to Paris, 'incandescent with rage': 'I had to write – he would later explain – if I didn't, I would have exploded.'[19] The resulting text – 'Les Communistes et la Paix' – was one of his most passionate. In it, he defended the right to protest and defended the recourse to (politically motivated) violence, on the basis that such violence was in fact the product of, and the reaction against, the constant violence exercised by the oppressor (the state) against the oppressed. Thereafter he would often employ this argument – most notoriously in his 1961 preface to Frantz Fanon's *Les Damnés de la terre*.

One is nevertheless entitled to marvel at the passion deployed by Sartre in defence of a party that had spent the last ten years insulting, denigrating and slandering him. The explanation is probably as much psychological as it is political. In their defiance of the police ban, the Communists had demonstrated their contempt for bourgeois legitimacy; they had, in any case, been outside of the democratic process since their rejection of the Marshall Plan. Elsewhere, the House Un-American Activities Committee was in full hue and cry (it would have its finest hour with the execution of the Rosenbergs in 1953), and the revelation of the Soviet camps in 1950 had further contributed to the embattled position of the PCF. All of these factors enabled Sartre to cast the erstwhile bully as the new victim. Even so, what is most striking about 'Les Communistes et la Paix' is less its impassioned defence of the Communists than the violence of its attack on the bourgeoisie. Sartre later recalled: 'I swore a hatred for the bourgeoisie that will accompany me to the grave.'[20] These two elements – the championing of the underdog and the unconditional hatred of the bourgeoisie – were, of course, hardly new: hatred of the bourgeoisie oozes off every page of *La Nausée*, and since 1944 Sartre's sympathy had gone instinctively to the oppressed: blacks, Jews, workers, colonized peoples etc. But from 1952 these visceral inclinations take on the appearance of a system. Sartre has sometimes been accused by commentators of inconsistency, or even incoherence, in the political stances he adopted, but the underlying system is perfectly coherent and it can be stated quite boldly: whatever the struggle, the only side that one can take is that of the oppressed. This enables the intellectual to act, secure in the knowledge that his actions are justified by an ethical certainty. The ethics that Sartre had failed to *write* now became an ethics of praxis.

The opposition between oppressor and oppressed can be seen to underlie the most ostensibly diverse of political positions; thus, he will support the Hungarians and the Czechs against the Soviet tanks, the Cubans against the USA, the Algerians against the French, the Palestinians against the Israelis, the Israelis against their regional aggressors, the students against their professors, the patient against his analyst, the Maoists against the French state; indeed, *anyone* against the bourgeois state.

Or at least from 1956 he would. In 1952–56 Sartre was a 'critical fellow-traveller' of the PCF. During these years he did not permit himself a single word or a single act that could be construed as anti-Communist. Much of what he did and said at this period was ill-judged, but nevertheless comprehensible within the context of the Cold War. (Critics of Sartre's supposed 'Stalinism' at this period might care to know that a young Michel Foucault chose 1950 as the moment to become a card-carrying member of the Party.) The most public display of unanimity with the Communists was the Vienna Peace Congress of 1952 – convened by the World Peace Movement, but largely stage-managed by the Communists. It was in Vienna that he acted to ban future performances of *Les Mains sales* lest the play be used as anti-Communist propaganda. The real pleasure that he took in feeling himself part of a mass movement did not blind him to the fact that he was being manipulated – not for the first time, and certainly not for the last. Neither did it blind him to the superficiality of his relations with his new comrades: 'I was dealing with men who considered only party members as comrades, men whose minds were stuffed with orders and prohibitions, who considered me as a temporary fellow-traveller and who were already anticipating the moment when I'd drop out of the fight and be recuperated by the forces of the right.'[21] The new 'friends' hardly compensated for the loss of the old: as Sartre perversely moved closer to the Communists, others were flocking in the other direction. There were significant departures from *TM* – not least Merleau-Ponty – and there was one particularly public falling-out.

Sartre and Camus had not, perhaps, had the closest of friendships, with several ruptures and periods of coolness throughout the 1940s. There had been a momentary *rapprochement* in 1951, but the truce ended abruptly a year later. In autumn 1951 Camus had published *L'Homme révolté* – a book that placed him firmly in the anti-Communist camp and which preached a kind of 'moral revolt' in the place of revolution, while condemning any recourse to violence in the pursuit of social justice. Sartre and his colleagues at *TM* regarded the book as reactionary and poorly argued. Sartre thought it best not to review it, largely out of a vestigial regard for Camus himself. For fully six months this silence was maintained; eventually the silence of *TM* became more eloquent than a review – no matter how negative – would have been. One of Sartre's collaborators, Francis Jeanson, bit the bullet in May 1952 and published a highly critical review of the book. Camus responded haughtily – not to Jeanson, but over his head to 'Monsieur le Directeur des *Temps Modernes*'. Finally, Sartre was forced to take up his pen, which he did to devastating effect. His response, coupled with an even harsher one from Jeanson, ominously entitled *'Pour tout vous dire . . .'* ('To be absolutely frank . . .'), completed what was tantamount to a literary assassination. The two former friends never met or spoke again. However, when Camus died in a car-crash in 1960, Sartre wrote a short but moving homage to him. If the so-called *Querelle* (literary dispute) between the two men continues even now to engage the interest of commentators,[22] it is partly because their positions (pro/anti-Communist) were emblematic, but also because the dispute was conducted at a remarkably high level of argument and rhetoric. Less obviously, the dispute was also fuelled by significant personal differences. The pampered child of the Luxembourg Gardens and the street urchin of Algiers crystallized a series of oppositions: bourgeois/working-class; metropolis/colony; Academe/the 'school of life'; ugly/handsome . . . There is no doubt that Sartre suffered most from these comparisons: like it or not, the accidents of Camus's birth gave him a kind of credibility that Sartre could never hope to achieve. Finally, unlike Sartre, Camus had once been a member of the Communist party.

In 1954 Sartre's new friends invited him for a protracted visit – the first of many – to the USSR. He was at least attempting to put more than just his armchair in the direction of history.[23] In the event, the visit nearly cost him his life. The month-long visit saw him whisked frenetically between Moscow, Leningrad and South Central Asia – wined, dined, fêted and propagandized wherever he went. The trip was not dissimilar to the one he had undertaken ten years earlier to the USA, except that the large quantities of bourbon were replaced by even larger quantities of vodka. The overwork, the alcohol, the tobacco took their toll and he collapsed and spent ten days in a Soviet hospital being treated for an attack of hypertension. On his return in June 1954 he remained severely weakened, but this alone cannot fully explain the panegyrics he published on his return. One interview was published under the snappy title: 'Freedom to criticise is total in the USSR, and the Soviet citizen is ceaselessly improving his condition within a society in continual progress.' This was the Soviet Union in 1953 . . . In an interview towards the end of his life he averred: 'Ah yes, hmm, that's right, after my first visit to the USSR in 1954, I lied. Well, "lied" is perhaps putting it too strongly: I wrote an article . . . in which I said some nice things about the USSR that I didn't really believe.'[24]

It is interesting that truth and lies figure prominently in Sartre's only two literary works of 1952–59. Both of these works have a professional 'liar' as their central character. Sartre's *Kean* – somewhat neglected by critics because it was 'merely' an adaptation of a nineteenth-century drama – can be seen in retrospect to be a pivotal work. On the face of it, the play has little to do with Sartre's outward preoccupations of the moment: it was premiered in 1953, at the height of his 'fellow-travelling' with the PCF. Dumas's original had turned on the problems of social integration of its protagonist: the actor Edmund Kean is caught in a social limbo between his poor origins and disreputable profession, on the one hand, and, on the other, the glittering world of the Court to which his talents, and the patronage of the Prince of Wales, give him access. He was a character after Sartre's own heart: an orphan, a bastard, an outsider-insider: a traitor. The *monstre sacré* of the English theatre, he was clearly also a monster in the Sartrean sense of the term. Yet the play explores a different side to his monstrosity, for he is also a geek, a fairground attraction for the rich and powerful: 'Serious men need illusions . . . So what do they do? They take a child and they turn him into an optical illusion [*trompe-l'œil*].'[25]

Philosophically, the play is informed by *L'Etre et le néant* and even earlier works such as *L'Imaginaire*. In the latter work Sartre had discussed the paradox of the actor: the actor does not 'make a character real' on stage; rather, he 'de-realizes' *himself* in the character which, in turn, is sustained by the imagination and belief (or willing suspension of disbelief) of the audience. He thus *depends* – ontologically – on the goodwill of the audience. But this paradox is shown in *L'Etre et le néant* to be universal: if we *are* nothing, then we must play at being what we are. Viewed with the benefit of hindsight, *Kean* is probably the most 'truthful' work of this period. It is hard to resist the thought that the portrait of this living *trompe-l'œil* is in some measure a self-portrait: 'I am a false prince, a false minister, a false general. Apart from that, I'm nothing. Oh yes, I forgot: a national glory . . . For twenty years I've been performing *gestures* to please you; can you understand that I might want to *act?*' Since he came to prominence in 1945, Sartre had never been out of the public eye. As he began to 'perform on the world stage' in the 1950s, he must have begun to wonder where his own reality lay. In 1952–56, when he was effectively lending his body and his persona to the Communists, the sense of a divorce between the public and the private spheres became even more acute. One could note in this connection that 1953 also saw the commencement of three huge undertakings: the autobiography (*Les Mots*), *Critique de la raison dialectique,* and the monstrous biography of Flaubert (*L'Idiot de la famille*). The massive personal investment represented by these works was quite invisible to the outside world: it was for example, nearly twenty years before the *Idiot* saw the light of day. Having said that, Sartre had always been aware of this divorce – both as an inescapable entailment of the human condition and as an element of the sensibility of the writer.

The other play of this period was *Nekrassov*. It was a fairly crude satire on the machinations of the bourgeois popular press and has a confidence trickster as its central character. Whilst in one way the play is clearly dated (it is a kind of *Pravda* of the 1950s), its theme of illusion clearly links it to the broader preoccupations just outlined with reference to *Kean*: 'the con-man, like the actor, is a professional of appearance and counterfeit'.[26]

The period of fellow-travelling ended as abruptly as it had begun. Sartre was again in Rome, in the autumn of 1956, when he heard that the Soviet tanks had crushed the Hungarian uprising. His reaction was immediate and characteristic: siding with the

Simone de Beauvoir and Sartre at rehearsal of Sartre's *Nekrassov* at the Théâtre Antoine, Paris, 1955.

underdog, he unreservedly condemned the Soviet aggression and brought an end to the *rapprochement* in the most unequivocal of fashions: 'I say that it is not possible, and never will be possible to renew relations with the men who are in charge of the PCF at the moment. Every sentence, every gesture is the culmination of thirty years of lies and sclerosis.'[27]

Those years of fellow-travelling were not all discussions about tractors and combine harvesters with men in shirt-sleeves in smoke-filled rooms: the incestuous complexity of Sartre's love-life was also being further enriched. In 1955 he met the actress and militant Evelyne Rey. She was the sister of Beauvoir's lover Claude Lanzmann (who was also on the editorial board of *TM*). They would remain close until Rey's suicide in 1966. In 1956 Sartre started a friendship with an eighteen-year-old student, Arlette El Kaïm, which would last 24 years. In 1965 he legally adopted her and later made her his literary executor. After his death, she oversaw the publication of most of the major posthumous works. What is perhaps surprising is the way he compartmentalized his love-life, and the fact that the women so readily accepted this (the exception, of course, had been Dolorès: one reason for their break-up was that she had no intention of being just another one of 'Sartre's women'). In the 1950s he often had up to five concurrent partners, each allotted their own time and space: a miracle of 'time management'! Occasionally they would intersect, as in 1959, when he wrote the two female roles of *Les Séquestrés d'Altona* specifically for two former lovers, Wanda and Evelyne.

For the rest of the decade, and beyond, Sartre lent himself – wholeheartedly this time – to anti-colonial struggles. After 1955 his name became virtually synonymous with the cause of Algerian independence, winning for him the admiration and esteem of many,

Sartre and Arlette El Kaïm in the 1960s.

and the bitter and potentially murderous enmity of others. The nationalist uprising in Algeria had begun in earnest in late 1954. Predictably, the French government had dismissed the *fellaghas* of the *Front de Libération Nationale* (FLN) as a minority of 'outlaws' and 'criminals'. But very quickly a number of French intellectuals started to publish carefully researched articles and reportages demonstrating the moral bankruptcy of France's colonial adventure in Algeria and the justice of the FLN's cause. The articles – and, notably, Francis Jeanson's book *L'Algérie hors la loi* (*Outlaw Algeria*) – began to influence public opinion in France, but the brutal repression conducted by French paratroopers showed no sign of being sensitive to public opinion. In 1955 Sartre had joined the Action Committee of intellectuals opposed to the war in Algeria, and at a large public meeting in early 1956 he made a significant contribution to the cause. Giving so many public lectures and interviews over the years, Sartre tended on occasion to be less than perfectly prepared, less than totally rigorous, but the lecture he delivered that night was a powerful, tightly argued and well-documented indictment of *L'Algérie française*. In the course of arguing for a peaceful end to the conflict and the granting of independence to Algeria, he returned to a theme that was a constant in his treatment of the Self and the (colonial) Other: colonialism is a system that mutilates its perpetrators almost as much as its victims: colonialism colonizes the colonizer. This means that the struggle of the independence movements is also, paradoxically, a struggle to free all men, including their oppressors. A formulation of this idea was given in the 1961 preface to Fanon's book referred to earlier: 'We Europeans are being de-colonised too: that means that the colonialist in each of us is being ripped out by means of a bloody operation.'[28] By 1957, with the appearance of ever more testimony from traumatized conscripts and victims, the systematic use of torture in Algeria had become the burning issue. Sartre's most decisive journalistic intervention on this question was a 1957 article, addressed to a French public, and entitled '*Vous êtes formidables*'. In it, Sartre contrasted the 'feel-good' atmosphere of a population smugly enjoying the early benefits of the consumer boom with the horrors that were perpetrated in their name in Algeria. This was followed in 1958 by a passionate and polemical article on the subject of Henri Alleg's *La Question*. In that work, Alleg had described the torture to which he had been subjected the year before. The title of the article ('Une victoire') refers to the triumph of the victim who affirms his humanity by not only surviving the torture, but also by relating it – thus saving *us all* from despair and shame.

In 1958 Sartre came close to killing himself: he was working so furiously that he nearly wrote himself into an early grave. Whilst working round the clock to finish *Critique de la raison dialectique*, he also wrote a long play and the first draft of a huge screenplay for John Huston. He also made numerous public interventions on Algeria. All of this was fuelled by increased abuse of alcohol, tobacco and, above all, amphetamines. From the 1940s Sartre had supplemented his consumption of alcohol and tobacco with commercially available stimulants, but in the 1950s the preferred drug became Corydrane – a cocktail of aspirin and amphetamine. Sartre, of course, habitually exceeded the recommended dose in an attempt to sharpen his thought processes, or simply to stay awake.

A year that had begun badly ended even worse: de Gaulle returned from self-imposed exile in Lorraine and, like some grotesque *deus ex machina* (and like Pétain before him), modestly offered to save France from itself. Despite Sartre's best efforts to sway public opinion, the General was confirmed in power by the referendum of September of that year. The Fourth Republic was 'saved' by being abolished and replaced by the Fifth, and de Gaulle swiftly set about fashioning the constitution in his image – with greatly increased presidential powers. In the event, the General proved infinitely more flexible and pragmatic in his solution to the Algerian conflict than anyone could have imagined.

The first literary fruits of this *annus horribilis* were born in 1959 with the production of *Les Séquestrés d'Altona*. Excepting his 1965 adaptation of Euripides' *Trojan Women*, this was to be Sartre's farewell to the theatre. It is a dark and difficult play. With a running time in excess of four hours, it also verges on the unstageable. The play is set in a family of powerful German industrialists dominated by the archly-named Father. The revelation around which the action turns is that the heir to the business – Frantz – had tortured partisans while fighting on the Eastern Front in World War II. He now spends his life sequestrated in his room, justifying himself and his century before posterity, the latter taking the form of a tribunal of thirtieth-century crabs. Although the play works perfectly well as a discussion of torture, guilt and national responsibility in the context of a resurgent Germany, it had other resonances that were not lost on a contemporary audience: for the Nazis, read the French, and for the Eastern Front, read Algeria. It is Sartre's most complex play, exploring the nature of torture and debating the role of violence in history. Philosophically, it draws heavily on the *Critique*. In the portrayal of the Father, it also seems to have a deeply pathological strain.

The Father was the subject of the screenplay mentioned earlier. John Huston wished to make a film about Freud centred on the 'heroic years': the battles against the medical establishment and anti-Semitism, the self-analysis and the 'discovery' of the talking-cure. He was, bizarrely, under the impression that Sartre 'knew Freud's work inside out'. I say this is bizarre because Sartre had spent the last twenty years vehemently denying the very existence of the unconscious and had read only a fraction of Freud's vast opus. As it happened, Sartre's accountant had not been keeping up with his tax returns and Sartre was, effectively, 'broke'. The $20,000 that Huston offered – chicken-feed by Hollywood standards, even in 1959 – may well have influenced Sartre's decision to accept the project. Sartre himself later claimed that this was the

Serge Reggiani and Marie Olivier (Wanda Kosakiewicz's professional name) in Sartre's *Les Séquestrés d'Altona* at the Théâtre de la Renaissance, Paris, September 1959.

sole motivating factor, but that claim is as dubious as it is revealing. To say that Sartre and Huston did not see eye to eye would be something of an understatement. The history of their mutual incomprehension – told in Huston's autobiography and in Sartre's letters to Beauvoir, and later interviews – could fill a chapter on its own. One could say that Sartre had problems with the medium: asked to make cuts to his first draft, he produced a second draft that would have taken eight hours of screen time! When Huston brought in professional screenwriters to make the cuts, Sartre withdrew his name from the credits. The film was released in 1962 under the title *Freud: The Secret Passion* and features a mesmerizing performance by Montgomery Clift in the title role. In fact, the finished film retains not only the basic structure Sartre had created, but also much of the emphasis he had given to the material. In view of the centrality of the father in the *Séquestrés*, it is striking that Sartre structured his screenplay around Freud's liquidation of a succession of powerful father-figures, against the ever-present backdrop of his relationship with his actual father, Jacob. At the end of the synopsis, Freud himself becomes the Father – albeit a symbolic one – aware of the role he must now play in the eyes of his disciples.[29]

It is worth pausing to note that father–son relationships (real or symbolic) had been a major preoccupation in Sartre's work from the juvenilia onwards, but previously the Son had always triumphed over the Father. It is not easy to see why the father-figure becomes vested with such sinister power in the work of the late 1950s. The theme did not go unnoticed by contemporary commentators: one ill-intentioned critic suggested that the virulence of Sartre's attacks on de Gaulle was due to what he called Sartre's 'father complex'. Whilst malicious, and technically approximate, the suggestion probably contains a grain of truth; after all, de Gaulle systematically presented himself as the 'father of the nation': the good father or the bad father, depending on one's politics. But for Sartre, precisely, that alternative did not exist: 'There is no good father. It's the rule.'[30]

5

No More the Universal Intellectual

In 1960 Sartre was at the very height of his fame, and this fame was truly global. At the start of that year he and Beauvoir were invited to Cuba to witness a revolution in action. His only previous visit had been in 1949, when the island was a gigantic gambling and prostitution racket run by Batista and the American Mafia. Ten years on, the transformation could not have been more radical. In France, Sartre had been mired in the increasingly depressing endgame of the Algerian war and he needed to believe that, somewhere, hope was still alive. Cuba fulfilled that need in every respect: this was still the 'honeymoon' of the revolution. What he found particularly alluring about the Cuban revolutionaries was their youth (long a privileged theme in Sartre): the average age of the ministers in the revolutionary government was less than 29; that and the fact that the revolution appeared to be largely 'improvised': here, for once, was a revolution where ideology seemed to grow organically out of revolutionary praxis. He would find these two elements again ten years later during his involvement with the French Maoists. Moreover, Cuba was an underdog: here was another third-world David slaying the imperialist Goliath.

He and Beauvoir spent a month on the island in February-March, often in the company of Che Guevara and Fidel himself. It is unlikely that Castro and 'El Che' felt they had anything to learn from the European intellectuals: Sartre was there to give his official sanction to the revolution; this was an exercise in what we would now call 'mediatization'. And sanction it he did, in a series of sixteen articles published in the popular French daily *France-Soir* in June-July of that year. The collective title of these reports is 'Ouragan sur le sucre' ('Hurricane over the sugar-cane'), but they were not exactly written by Sartre himself: he had begun a massive study of the Cuban revolution while there – the extant manuscript runs to 1,100 pages – and the reportages were extracted from those notes and 'tidied up' by Claude Lanzmann, then a journalist on *France-Dimanche*. The articles painted a wholly enthusiastic and romanticized picture of the revolution, which is not to say that Sartre subscribed entirely to that vision: not for the first time, he allowed the imperative of support for a cause to override the desire for objectivity. Honeymoons do not last, and only nine months later, when passing back through Cuba, he noted the hardening of the regime in the face of external hostility. Sartre never authorized the republication in France of those articles, but they were published in Spanish in a volume entitled *Sartre visitá a Cuba* that was widely read in Latin America and the Caribbean. Even today, copies can be found for a few pesos in the second-hand bookshops of Havana's Plaza de la Catedral, alongside dusty volumes of Marx and Lenin.

Sartre had only been back in Paris for a few months before he responded to a second invitation from the Americas; this time it was the Brazilian writer and militant Jorge Amado who invited him for a prolonged stay in that country. The visit lasted from mid-August to the end of September and was regarded by Sartre as the prolongation of his trip to Cuba. Apart from touring the country extensively, he gave numerous public lectures and interviews. This trip was publicized and politicized even more than the visit to Cuba. One needs to appreciate that Sartre had become a truly international figure – the 'symbolic intellectual', as Cohen-Solal put it: photographs of Sartre with Castro and Che were published not only in Cuba but almost daily back in France, and worldwide; speeches made in Havana or Saõ Paolo were not only for local consumption, but were reproduced the world over: Sartre was talking to a global audience. No intellectual, before or since, has ever reached such a wide public. His fame had made him, effectively, untouchable, and he exploited his status to the full. The previous year, Malraux (now de Gaulle's Minister of Culture) had made an official trip to Brazil and had promoted the government line on *Algérie française*; Sartre was determined to undo the work of his predecessor. Obsessively and repeatedly, he drew together Cuba, Brazil and Algeria, informing his audiences about the war in Algeria, drawing parallels with their own situation. The message was clear: colonization – or economic 'post-colonialism' – was an evil and must be combated wherever it existed, be it in Africa, the Caribbean, Southeast Asia or Latin America. The Algerians and the Cubans had shown the way: the fight was there to be won.

So well reported were Sartre's activities in Brazil that his friends feared for his safety were he to return directly to Paris. On their advice he flew back to Barcelona and regained Paris uneventfully, by car. But it was not only Sartre's inflammatory speeches that had sparked fears for his safety. In at least one way, the trip to Brazil had been badly timed: in 1957 Francis Jeanson had organized a support network for FLN militants in France; the network had been detected and broken up, its organisers arrested, and on 5 September 1960 the trial of Jeanson and his comrades opened before a military tribunal in Paris. To coincide with the start of the trial, a petition supporting the right to *insoumission* (insubordination or the refusal to take orders) in Algeria was published. The text of the manifesto – signed by 121 leading writers, intellectuals, academics, reporters and journalists, including Sartre of course – ended with words that echo Sartre's long-held view that the struggles of the oppressed were waged for the benefit of *all*: 'the cause of the Algerian people, which is making a decisive contribution to the destruction of the colonial system, is the cause of all free men'. Sartre had not organized the petition, but his presence amongst the signatories, like his presence in Cuba and Brazil, was a further instance of his totemic status.

The trial was a fiasco for the French army: if they had actively sought to incite debate about the use of torture, about the massacre of civilians, about the legality or otherwise of the French presence in Algeria, they could not have done better. Accuser turned into accused as the army and the government found themselves the subject of repeated, detailed indictments from the witnesses. But Sartre, of course, was not there: he was in Brazil. By way of testimony, he sent a letter that was a blatant provocation, defending the FLN and their supporters and attacking the government. Ironically, Sartre did not even write the letter himself: he had indicated by telephone what he wanted to say and it had been written by two of his collaborators from *TM*, and his signature expertly forged.

Sartre was, effectively, daring de Gaulle to arrest him, but the challenge was not accepted – the president famously declaring that 'one does not arrest Voltaire!' (Voltaire was, of course, arrested; he was also thrashed by the lackeys of the noble he had offended, although it is not clear whether or not de Gaulle had that in mind.) Others, however, were punished: state employees – including academics and civil servants – who had signed the so-called 'Manifesto of the 121' were sacked, as were journalists and employees of the state media. The implication of de Gaulle's tactic of dealing differently with intellectuals and employees of the state was clear: only the former had the right to a conscience.

The Algerian war officially ended with the ratification by referendum of the Evian agreements in April 1962, but not before further bloodshed and massacres. A group of die-hard generals had attempted a putsch in Algiers in April and, in the wake of its failure, formed the Organisation Armée Secrète (OAS) which brought right-wing terrorism to the streets of Paris: already in October 1960 a crowd of 10,000 had marched in Paris chanting 'Shoot Sartre!'; now, two attempts were made to blow up Sartre's flat (in July 1961

Sartre being interviewed by journalists during the Algerian War.

and January 1962) and the offices of *TM* were damaged by a blast in May 1961. All of this confirms that Sartre's position on Algeria was perceived to be more than mere intellectual posturing!

Sartre may have slept through the Popular Front, tergiversated during the Spanish Civil War and eschewed direct action in the Resistance, but he did not 'miss' Algeria: despite the fact that he perhaps followed more than he led, Algeria was certainly 'Sartre's war'.

It was not only political interventions that thrust Sartre into the limelight in 1960. In April of that year, between his visits to Cuba and Brazil, he had finally published the great philosophical work of his mature years – or what he took to be so. Like *L'Etre et le néant* before it, *Critique de la raison dialectique* had been ten years in the making. Sartre's practical *rapprochement* with the Communists in the early 1950s had been accompanied by the start of an attempt on his part to arrive at a theoretical synthesis between Existentialism and Marxism. A century earlier, the Danish philosopher Kierkegaard had affirmed, against the totalizing system of Hegel, the irreducibility and the specificity of lived experience; now, Sartre was attempting to achieve a rational synthesis of this subjectivity, which is the start-ing point of any Existentialism, and the objectivity of the method of dialectical Materialism. He saw himself as rescuing what was most valuable in Marx's thought from the 'laziness' of what passed for Marxist theory within the PCF. The 'lazy Marxist' will see men as mere objects in a world of objects; he will, for example, negate the subjectivity of a poet like Paul Valéry with a dismissive observation such as 'Valéry was a petit-bourgeois intellectual.' That is, every-thing Valéry wrote, did or felt could be deduced from this 'objective' observation. But, as Sartre points out, 'Valéry is a petit-bourgeois intellectual, of that there is no doubt. But not every petit-bourgeois intellectual is Paul Valéry.'[1] The task that he set himself was immense: he was trying to save contemporary Marxism from itself by giving it the ontological foundation it lacked.

L'Etre et le néant had deployed a quarter of a million words in its demonstration of man's fundamental ontological freedom, and the *Critique* takes as third as many words again in its attempt to understand why, in that case, the social world is characterized by *alienation* and *opacity*. The culprit is man himself – always 'making himself' but under 'conditions that are not of his own making': 'History is more complex than a certain simplistic Marxism would have it, and man does not only have to struggle against Nature, against the social milieu that engendered him, against other men, but also against his own action in so far as it becomes *other*.'[2]

The work contains a number of memorable descriptions: the 'bus queue', used to illustrate the notion of seriality; the storming of the Bastille as an instance of the 'group-in-fusion'; the birth of 'fraternity-terror' in the Tennis Court oath . . . but these never entered even the periphery of popular consciousness in the way that the café waiter or 'my friend Pierre' from *L'Etre et le néant* had done. The *Critique* is a very long and very difficult book. It was read, and even quite well reviewed – by philosophers at least – but by a relatively small group of specialists. The anthropologist

Claude Lévi-Strauss, whilst having serious reservations about the book, took it seriously enough to ask Sartre's collaborator on *TM*, Jean Pouillon, to conduct a semester-long seminar on it at the Ecole Pratique des Hautes Etudes in 1961. Michel Foucault famously described it as 'the magnificent and pathetic effort of a man of the nineteenth century to think the twentieth.'[3]

By Sartre's own admission, the writing of the *Critique* was 'not pretty'.[4] By this, he was referring to the style, and he excused it on methodological grounds: if the text contained so many prolix periods with multiple sub-clauses held together by a string of 'inasmuch as' and 'insofar as', it was because the dialectical method required it. But the writing in the physical sense was not pretty either. He had written all 390,000 words in 1958–59, fuelled by the usual cocktail of alcohol, tobacco and amphetamines; not surprisingly, the manuscript is somewhat difficult to decipher. Just as *L'Etre et le néant* had ended with the promise of an Ethics to follow, so the *Critique* ended with the announcement of a second volume on the 'intelligibility of history'. Neither was ever completed, though the notes and drafts for both were published after Sartre's death.

Ever since the death of his stepfather in 1945, Sartre had shared a flat with his mother at 42, rue Bonaparte on the Left Bank, but after the second OAS attack in January 1962 he moved into a tenth-floor studio flat at 222, boulevard Raspail in Montparnasse, bringing the Saint-Germain-des-Prés era to an end. His mother moved into a small hotel nearby. Life returned to what passed for normality: holidays in Italy, three trips to the Soviet Union, two meetings with Khrushchev . . . but Sartre was no longer a starry-eyed sovietophile: his sympathies lay henceforth with the liberals and the dissidents of that country. In 1963 his public image was that of the globe-trotting activist and scourge of the political establishment – after all, he had produced nothing in the way of literature in the previous ten years save two plays, and the last of those had been back in 1959. So the publication in *TM* in October-November 1963, and then in volume form in 1964, of a highly literary autobiography, of all things, was greeted with amazement and not a little delight – for once right across the political spectrum.

It is now known that Sartre had started work on his own autobiography in 1952 in the wake of the publication of *Saint Genet*. It has been remarked that Sartre's bursts of autobiographical activity coincided with moments of crisis or transformation; this was the case with the self-portrait written during the Phoney War, and it appears to be the case in 1952–56 when Sartre had momentarily turned himself into a 'critical fellow-traveller' of the PCF. But it is only half the story: another explanation for the autobiographical activity of the early 1950s is to be found in the nature of the work he had carried out on Genet. Childhood was an important focus of the Genet book, and it certainly appears that Sartre was now prepared to give more weight to the alienating effect of childhood than had previously been the case. Readers of *L'Etre et le néant* could have been forgiven for supposing that men were 'born at the age of twenty-five and entered the world with a memory but without a personal experience to account for it'.[5] Having long criticized the Freudian emphasis on childhood in the formation of the personality, Sartre seems now to have drawn inspiration from the 'French Freud': in the *Cahiers pour une morale*, he discusses Jacques Lacan's article in the *Encyclopédie Française* on 'Les complexes familiaux dans la formation de l'individu', and notes: 'There is another kind of alienation (and it is capital) found in all societies: it is that of the child.'[6] We know from surviving manuscripts and notes that Sartre had at first planned to write an intellectual history of his generation, but that the focus had gradually narrowed to his own childhood. The problem was: when did childhood end? In the event, he chose a significant cut-off point: the remarriage of his mother in 1917.

A page from the final manuscript of Sartre's *Les Mots*, 1963.

It is extremely difficult to say anything about *Les Mots* that does not need immediately to be hedged round with provisos and qualifications, and this for two main reasons. Towards the end of the book Sartre produces a phrase that summarizes its whole movement: 'I was fleeing, external forces modelled my flight and made me.'[7] That is to say, the vision he develops is a dialectical one. Sartre imagined the dialectic as a spiral: an argument that goes round in circles but which is constantly shifting up to the next level of analysis; every time a synthesis is achieved, it becomes, in turn, the thesis that inaugurates the next round. This means that, at any given moment, any assertion the author might make (about himself) is only provisionally true: true subjectively, but false objectively, and vice versa. This is the meaning of the unexpected remark that occurs 50 pages into the narration: 'Everything I have just written is false. True. Neither true nor false, like everything one writes about madmen, about men.'[8] A second difficulty lies in the style of the writing. As the manuscripts prove, this was the most intensively 'worked on' of all of Sartre's texts. The philosophical and theoretical texts were normally written in a continuous outpouring with very few crossings-out or amendments. The literary texts were visibly subject to considerable stylistic honing and polishing. But *Les Mots* stands out even amongst the latter: many manuscript pages contain just a single sentence, crossed through and rewritten on the next page with alterations and, often, greatly expanded, but sometimes also contracted. This means that every single word of the text was scrutinized and carefully weighed for its effect. The result is dazzling: pastiche, parody, irony, humour, puns – a veritable compendium of rhetorical figures. But what was the purpose of all of this stylistic labour? Sartre's own explanation is not entirely convincing: 'I wanted [this book] to be more literary than the others, because I considered it to be, as it were, a farewell to literature . . . I wanted to be literary in order to demonstrate the error of being literary.'[9] But if this were the case, he could have chosen any language (technical, popular etc.) for the purposes of the demonstration – or simply kept quiet (like Rimbaud). In any case, the end of the book makes it clear that he is *not* yet done with writing.[10] A more convincing answer is suggested by Sartre's views on the nature of style itself. In a 1970s interview he remarked: 'language that does not say what it is talking about is *style*. Style is not just a way of saying what one has to say, but a way of not saying what one does not have to say.'[11] For the most part, when critics declared the style of *Les Mots* to be 'dazzling' and 'brilliant', they were unaware of the literal truth of what they were saying. The 'I' that speaks itself in the text is ultimately little more than a rhetorical effect: one long oxymoron. One could further suggest that it was this very realization that prompted the writing of the work in the first place. Sartre starts from an admission of failure: he knows that he can never reply to the question 'Who am I?' with anything more than words that will never coincide with the unknowable truth. At best, the relation between language and truth might be 'asymptotic'. Most readers affected to take *Les Mots* at face value and chose to see it as the distillation of those qualities that seemed synonymous with French literature: wit, charm and profundity.

As if they had been laying in wait for him, the Swedish Academy pounced and promptly awarded Sartre the Nobel Prize for litera-ture in October 1964. And he refused it. The sequence of events was actually not quite that simple. Shortly before the announce-ment, Sartre had learnt that he was in the running and wrote to the Academy in order, as it were, to refuse it in advance. But the Swedes ignored the letter. Two days after the announcement, he published an explanation of his refusal in *Le Monde*. He cited 'personal' and 'objective' reasons. The personal reasons came down to a horror of institutionalization. He explained that he had always systematically declined any 'official' honours (such as the Légion d'honneur after the war) in order to remain fully independent: 'The writer must refuse to allow himself to be transformed into an institution.' The 'objective' reasons were also connected to inde-pendence. He tactfully suggested that his acceptance of the honour would doubtless have been used in ways which neither he nor the Swedish Academy would condone, in the context of the continuing confrontation between East and West. He further pointed out that he would have accepted the prize had it been awarded to him at the height of his involvement alongside the FLN, but the fact that the Academy had waited until he was politically 'safe' again, suggested to him that Nobel Prizes for literature are not always awarded on literary merit alone. Inevitably, his decision was denounced by politically hostile commentators as capricious and incoherent, but – psychologically as well as politically – it was entirely coherent. Sartre strove very hard to resist any kind of 'recuperation' by bourgeois society – he was the black sheep who would never return to the fold; psychologically, the narcissist could never lower himself to being elevated in this way: like Groucho Marx, he refused to join any club that would have him as a member . . . His only regret, it seems, was the large sum of money that went with it: it could have been donated to a good political cause, such as the anti-Apartheid movement, with which he had recently become involved.

To say, as I have, that Sartre had reached his peak in 1960 implies, thereafter, a decline. This decline was more tangible within France – always prone to intellectual fashions – than in the wider world, where he continued to enjoy enormous prestige. Even in the *Critique*, Sartre was still, in essence, working with the ontological models he had elaborated in the 1930s and 1940s. His intellectual power-base had been philosophy, and the privileged position of that discipline in French academe. But by 1960 the prestige of philosophy was waning. Reorganizations of the University system had given formal recognition to what became known as the *sciences humaines*: primarily, anthropology, sociology, psychology and linguistics. The vast intellectual field covered by Sartre's totalizing adventure was fragmenting into micro-disciplines practised by specialists with specialist skills. The new generation – those born after the war – had new intellectual *maîtres à penser*: Roland Barthes, *Le Degré zéro de l'écriture* (1953); *Mythologies* (1957); *Eléments de sémiologie* (1964); Claude Lévi-Strauss, *Anthropologie structurale* (1958); *La Pensée sauvage* (1962); Michel Foucault, *Folie et déraison: histoire de la folie à l'âge classique* (1961); *Les Mots et les Choses: une archéologie des sciences humaines* (1966); Louis Althusser, *Pour Marx* (1965); *Lire le Capital* (1965); Jacques Lacan, *Ecrits* (1966). Not to mention the young writers and theorists based around the review *Tel Quel* (founded in 1960). There were new kids on the block, but most were hardly 'kids': Lévi-Strauss was only three years younger than Sartre; Lacan was four years older. The exceptions here were Barthes and Foucault. This battle between old and new was pro-moted by the French media as the confrontation between Sartre and the Structuralists. In literature too, the Sartrean model of com-mitment was under attack. The *nouveaux romanciers* of the 1950s had explicitly theorized their own practice in opposition to that of Sartre, despite, in the case of Robbe-Grillet, acknowledging *La Nausée* as in some respects a forerunner of the *nouveau roman*.

There are many ironies in this, not least that *TM* had done more than any other publication to bring many of these writers and theorists to the attention of a wider public. Within *TM*'s editorial board, Jean-Bertrand Pontalis (himself an analyst) championed new psychoanalytic writing, whilst Jean Pouillon had long sought to recon-cile the structural anthropology of Lévi-Strauss and the 'synthetic anthropology' towards which Sartre had been striving. Nathalie Sarraute – a writer associated with the *nouveaux romanciers* – had virtually been launched by Sartre in the 1940s: her *Portrait d'un inconnu* found a publisher largely thanks to Sartre's personal efforts.

It is probably true that these 'new' writers and thinkers engaged – albeit critically – more with Sartre's work than he did with theirs. Herein lies one of Sartre's paradoxes: for a man who had always inhabited the world of ideas, he was strangely incurious about ideas that he sensed did not fit into his system. He had immersed himself in the phenomenology of Husserl and Heidegger but had assimilated it to his vision of the world, rather than being changed by it. He had discovered phenomenology thanks to the *Théorie de l'intuition dans la phénoménologie de Husserl* of his strict contempo-rary Emmanuel Levinas (seen today as a much more fashionable thinker than Sartre) but never engaged with him thereafter. The same could be said of his attitude to the work of his friend Merleau-Ponty (who is also, coincidentally, enjoying more serious critical attention than Sartre these days). Numerous interviewers attempted to provoke Sartre into a substantial debate with the new thinkers, but to little effect. When he was drawn into discussion, it often appeared that he had, at best, only a vague notion of what they had actually written. He had a standard, blanket dismissal of Structuralism in all its forms: 'structures' were simply part of what he called in the *Critique* the 'practico-inert', and were, as such, unintelligible unless taken up by human *praxis*; the Structuralists denied the very possibility of human agency; *he* regarded the human subject as cause, while *they* relegated it to the status of a mere discursive effect, etc. Sartre's evasiveness created the impression that he was 'past it', that he was locked in the past and no longer able to engage with what was most novel and vibrant in the realm of thought and letters. The era of the Universal Intellectual was over; the age of the specialist and the 'technician' had dawned.

Nevertheless, the writing of the *Critique* and the debate around the role of the intellectual that had been occasioned by the 'Structuralist controversy' led Sartre to reflect further on his own status as intellectual: what right had the intellectual to speak in the name of abstract, universal principles? In three lectures delivered in Japan in 1966 – but not published until 1972 – Sartre addressed precisely this question. He argues that the classic intellectual arose with the consolidation of bourgeois hegemony in the nineteenth century. The intellectual is recruited from that class and serves its interests, first as a 'technician of practical knowledge'. He becomes an intellectual when he starts to become involved in matters that do not concern him; and to do this, he must first become conscious of his own contradictions: he works in the name of values such as Truth, Objectivity and Universality, but the fruits of his labours are put to a *particular* use by the class that he serves – namely, the continuing hegemony of that class to the detriment of the under-classes who *labour* to realize those ends. Once awareness has dawned, he becomes – and the term will by now be familiar – a *monster*, or a 'man of contradictions'. The only way to avoid being paralysed by the contradiction between universality and particularity is for the intellectual to live that contradiction dialectically. This involves a process of continuous radicalization: the intellectual must intervene punctually, on specific issues of injustice, and must always place himself in the service of the masses. But he should be under no illusions: he will always be an outsider, the object of mistrust to the masses he tries to serve, and a traitor to the class that spawned him.

The problem itself is hardly new – it is the underlying subject of most of Sartre's major plays, especially *Les Mains sales* – but now he appears to recognize that it has no solution: the monster must live his monstrosity to the bitter end. He is thus a torn and solitary figure. One further task is incumbent upon him: he must subject himself to a continual process of self-examination, or *auto-critique*: this involves a reflexive extirpation of any assumptions, any habits of thought, any acquired certainties that may have taken root. The critic is essentially one who *separates* – the wheat from the chaff, for example – but he is also, in Sartre's notion of *auto-critique*, the one who separates himself from himself. The idea is not dissimilar to Lévi-Strauss's description of the acquisition of objective know-ledge, which requires the subject endlessly to split himself into subject and object, in a process of cumulative self-alienation. There is deep continuity at work here: Sartre had always intuited his own 'character' as being defined by 'de-solidarization': he had always betrayed, and dissociated himself from the self of yesterday in the name of the self he would become tomorrow. In the 25 years that separated the *Carnets de la drôle de guerre* from *Les Mots*, nothing had changed in this respect: 'I became a traitor and I have remained one. I can throw myself completely into an undertaking, give myself up unreservedly to a piece of work, to anger, to friendship, but in the very next instance I will disavow myself, I know it, I want it, and I betray myself already, in the very midst of my passion, by the joyful presentiment of my future betrayal.'[12] Sartre constitutes himself as a living paradox: the man whose only constancy lies in inconstancy; existence is a flight from the consistency of the self: the only time one is what one is, and everything one will ever be, is when one ceases to exist. In this sense, Sartre was a man who lived with death snapping at his heels.

As we will see, the last fifteen years of Sartre's life would provide ample opportunities for the 'punctual intervention' of the intellectual. But never had he led a more double life. There was an inside and an outside. The inside was the flat in Montparnasse: the 'family' and above all the female friends – Arlette, Beauvoir, Wanda, Michelle – Sunday lunch with his mother (until her death in 1969), his music, his piano . . . But above all his desk and the pool of light around the blank page slowly disappearing under the advancing tide of unruly black characters. Every day, the clock stood still and he had a rendezvous with another age, inhabited by a quite different kind of literary hermit: Gustave Flaubert. But there was also an outside, and here the clock never stopped.

Despite his numerous trips to the Soviet Union, Sartre maintained his highly critical stance on that regime, speaking out increasingly in favour of dissidents and denouncing the suppression of the 'Prague spring' as a 'war crime'. But this was not the only war crime that he denounced. In 1966, he had been invited to join the International Tribunal against War Crimes in Vietnam, organized by the venerable doyen of British philosophers, Bertrand Russell. He was elected its executive president in November of that year. The following spring, the Tribunal met in Stockholm, and again in Denmark in the autumn. At the end of World War II, once the last charged Nazi had been judged and dispatched, the Allies had made haste to dissolve the Nuremberg Tribunal lest their own actions fall foul of its justice. The legitimacy of the Russell Tribunal (as it became known), wrote Sartre, lay in its resurrection of a process begun at Nuremberg and now so conveniently forgotten. Today, in 2006, after Bosnia, after Rwanda, after Sudan and in the midst of Iraq, the concluding words of Sartre's write-up of the judgement of the Tribunal seem as urgent as ever:

> this crime . . . carried out every day before our very eyes, makes all those who do not denounce it the accomplices of those who perpetrate it, and, all the better to enslave us, it begins by degrading us. In this sense, imperialist genocide can only become more radical: for the group that it targets, through the Vietnamese nation, is the human group in its entirety.[13]

Today an International War Crimes Tribunal sits in The Hague; the USA does not recognize its legitimacy.

Sartre's other great public intervention of the late 1960s was the Arab–Israeli conflict, but in this conflict he found it impossible to take sides. He had been sensitized to the persecution of the Jews during World War II; he had been sympathetic to the Jewish terrorists in their struggle to oust the British and found the state of Israel, but he had also supported Nasser at the time of the Suez crisis, and the Algerian war had brought him many friends in the Arab world. Thus he maintained a stance of studied neutrality – which did not mean that he was blind to the rights and wrongs on both sides. With a view to fostering dialogue between Arabs and Israelis, he and Beauvoir undertook an 'official' trip to Egypt and Israel in 1967. It was not the moment for dialogue: only a few days after their return to France, the Six-Day War broke out. Sartre's loyalties are well expressed in an interview he had given to the Israeli newspaper *Al Hamishmar* in 1966: 'as the Arab world and Israel confront each other today, it is as if we are divided in our very selves, and we live this opposition as though it were our own personal tragedy.'[14] For the rest of his life, Sartre would maintain this neutrality, affirming both the right of the state of Israel to exist in security, and condemning its 'colonialist' attitude towards the Palestinians. It is significant that, on his death, Sartre was hailed as a friend both by the Israeli and by the Palestinian press.

The Vietnam War was an important element in the backdrop to the discontent that led to the student unrest across the world in 1967–68. In France, it began in a curiously Gallic manner: students in the Faculty of Nanterre protested at the absurd rule that barred male students from female halls of residence 'after hours', leading to violent confrontation with the University authorities and the police. But this was the random spark that ignited the power-keg: French students were thoroughly disillusioned with an outdated system in which 'knowledge' was handed down from on high by arrogant, out-of-touch professors in crumbling, over-crowded lecture theatres; they felt oppressed by an authoritarian and mediocre government held together by what amounted to a cult of personality around de Gaulle and supported by a quiescent mass media; and they felt angry about Vietnam. The unrest at Nanterre spread quickly to the Sorbonne, and barricades appeared in the Latin Quarter for the first time since the Commune of 1871. Violent confrontation with the notorious CRS (paramilitary riot police) followed. These students had no intellectual gurus – by and large, they regarded intellectuals as part of the problem – but they nevertheless invited Sartre to speak to them in the Grand Amphithéâtre of the Sorbonne, which they had occupied. His presence alone was sufficient to fill the room to overflowing, but few listened to what he said: once again, his presence was symbolic. For his part, Sartre saw in their revolt a cause that he must *necessarily* espouse: they were young, their adversaries were old, and they were fighting against the full force of an oppressive state. But it is not clear how well he *understood* them.

After the expulsion of the students from the Sorbonne, increasingly violently street-fighting over the barricades of the Left Bank

Sartre addressing an audience in 1968.

continued, eventually swaying public support in favour of the students, and provoking a spontaneous general strike. At this point, the government was close to falling, and perhaps even the state itself . . . But, with the help of the PCF – which revealed itself to be every bit as conservative as Sartre had long suspected – de Gaulle finally restored a semblance of order. Promises of reforms were made to the students; the trades unions – if not the workers them-selves – were bought off.

Unrest continued well into 1969. In February of that year Sartre spoke at a meeting held at the Mutualité (on the same platform as Michel Foucault) in support of 34 students expelled for their part in the unrest. As he prepared to speak, a young militant passed him a slip of paper which bore the words, using the familiar *tu* form of address: 'Sartre, keep it brief, keep it clear: we need to discuss what we're going to do!'

The street-fighting may have ceased, but this was not the end of '68. In its aftermath, numerous small, revolutionary groups – or *groupuscules* – were formed by young people who saw '68 as only the beginning, not the end, and who distrusted the Communists as much as they detested de Gaulle. One of these was the Gauche Prolétarienne (GP; it had actually been formed shortly *before* May '68), a revolutionary Maoist group dedicated to the continuation and radicalization of the struggle. Their newspaper, *La Cause du Peuple*, supported all forms of working-class revolutionary struggle – from workers protesting against sackings and lock-outs in France, to the Black Panthers in the USA. They very quickly came to the attention of the French authorities: in 1970 the newspaper's first two directors were arrested and imprisoned for their 'subversive activities'. Their colleagues had the idea of asking Sartre to take on the directorship of the newspaper, judging that the government would not dare imprison him. He was initially mystified: 'I hadn't quite understood what these young people wanted, nor had I understood what role an old buffer (*vieux con*) like me could play in that affair.'[15] But the 'old buffer' accepted, and subsequently took on the nominal directorship of up to a dozen far-left publications. But in the case of *La Cause du Peuple*, what was initially a mere cover became something more: Sartre started to debate with his young interlocutors and even genuinely edited two issues of the newspaper himself. When the authorities focused their efforts on the street-sellers of *La Cause du Peuple* – arresting them and often beating them up – Sartre, Beauvoir and others took to the streets to sell the paper themselves in an attempt to cause the police maximum discomfiture. They did arrest him, but he was quickly released by an embarrassed *commissariat*. Sartre's support for the Maoists and the causes they espoused was certainly more than symbolic – in his eyes at least. Which is not to say that he saw eye to eye with them on everything. He was careful not to give unconditional support to *any* action they might undertake, and was always wary of their clandestine armed faction. In the event, the GP dissolved itself in October 1973 realizing, in the wake of the successful creation of a workers' cooperative at the Lip factory, that the workers could actually manage quite well without them.

The years 1970–73 were probably the most politically intense of his life; he wished to incarnate the 'new intellectual', and the activities he undertook in these years certainly demonstrate what he understood by that term. He threw himself into the support of immigrant workers, protesting at their atrocious living conditions; he became involved in issues of workers' safety – especially in the mines; he protested against racism in the Goutte d'Or district of Paris; along with Foucault, he took up the cause for radical reform of the prison system; he launched enquiries into instances of police brutality and cover-ups – the most famous of these being the case of Pierre Overney, who had been shot dead by an armed guard at the state-owned Renault factory in Boulogne-Billancourt. Further afield, he took up the cause of Soviet Jews prevented from emigrating, whilst also writing a letter calling on Israel to cease persecuting conscientious objectors. In 1974, he made a visit to Andreas Baader, erstwhile leader of the Rote Armee Faktion, who was being held in solitary confinement in a German prison. Ill-health forced Sartre to reduce these kinds of 'punctual interventions' after 1975, but even as late as 1979 he turned out physically in support of the Vietnamese 'boat-people'.

There was one thing in particular about which Sartre and the young Maoists disagreed, and that was the work he was engaged upon. The militants had suggested that he could best support the workers by writing a popular novel! But Sartre would do no such thing; the work he had been writing, on and off, for nearly twenty years was nearing completion, and it was just about as far removed from a 'popular novel' as it was possible to imagine: volumes I and II of *L'Idiot de la famille* – an Existential biography of Gustave Flaubert – were published together in May 1971 and weighed in at over 1,500 pages; volume III was published the following year and brought the total to well in excess of 2,100 pages. Had not

Sartre once remarked that he had always regarded abundance as a virtue!

The question that Sartre poses at the start of *L'Idiot de la famille* is deceptively straightforward: 'What can one know about a man, today?' The 2,000 pages he produced were only the *beginnings* of a reply: at the point where the text ends, Sartre has not even arrived at the publication of Flaubert's first masterpiece, in his mid-thirties. The structure of the study is nonetheless quite straightforward: if the whole work is an amplification of the phrase 'you make yourself on the basis of what has been made of you', then the first volume reconstructs what was 'made of' Gustave as a child. The principal factors that contributed to Gustave's 'passivisation' were the relation to an adequate, but cold, mother – a mother who would perhaps not have been deemed 'good enough' by an analyst such as Winnicott; and to a stern, overbearing and prestigious father, as well as an older brother who attempted to be no more than a replica of his father. It is curious to read a Sartre who had so denigrated psychoanalysis in the 1940s and 1950s bemoaning the lack of information available on precisely how Caroline Flaubert had breast-fed and handled her baby son! The first volume, then, reconstructs the 'constitution': 'Such is Gustave. Such was he constituted. And, no doubt, there is no determination imprinted within a human being that he does not "go past" by and through his manner of living it.'[16] The second volume (*La Personnalisation*) is the history of this *dépassement* – or how Flaubert started to make himself on the basis of how he had been constituted by others. The third volume starts to explore Flaubert's choice of the imaginary as an expression, and a way out of the double-bind in which he had been placed. It contains an astonishingly long dialectical working-out of the multiple significances of a supposed epileptic fit suffered by Flaubert in the company of his brother at Pont L'Evêque: Sartre regards this 'falling fit' as the means 'invented' by Flaubert to transform a reality that was becoming unliveable (notably, it was a means of circumventing the familial expectation that he should 'adopt a profession').

L'Idiot is the most thorough application of the dialectical 'regressive–progressive' method. This involves a constant coming and going between past and future, between inside and outside: on the one hand, the subject is situated in his society, his milieu, his epoch, and, on the other, the project of the subject is grasped as he interiorizes and re-exteriorizes (in his actions, his creations etc.) the set of given conditions. This was Sartre's attempt – following on from *Critique de la raison dialectique* – to dissolve the opposition between subjectivity and objectivity in a truly dialectical movement that gives full weight to historical determination, whilst stopping short of erecting it as a final cause.

Looking back over Sartre's long list of existential biographical projects – which include some not mentioned here, such as the artist Tintoretto – certain patterns begin to emerge. In every case (except in that of Flaubert, where the mother is deficient), there is an exclusive relationship with an idealized mother; in every case, the idyll is shattered by a crushing father-figure. All of the subjects were artists of one kind or another (normally 'poets') and in each case, the central conundrum was why this subject chose the imaginary as the preferred escape from an existential crisis 'at the moment of suffocation'. If, as I suggested earlier, Sartre was seeking glimpses of his own reflection in these figures, one can ultimately only speculate on what he saw there. What is striking is the contrast between the immense 'will to know' that drove his biographical ventures, and the almost total ignorance that he professed with regard to his own father: 'About that man, nobody in my family has succeeded in making me curious.'[17] If the writing of the self, when pushed back far enough, always encounters a myth of origins, then it is perhaps significant that Jean-Baptiste remained largely a figure of myth for his son: 'I know him from hearsay, like the Man in the Iron Mask or the Chevalier d'Eon.'[18]

Worn down by years of overwork and sundry substance abuse, Sartre's health had long been in a parlous state. His heavy drinking and unhealthy diet (he particularly liked fatty pork dishes and charcuterie, and was virtually allergic to anything resembling a green vegetable) had left him with atherosclerosis, a condition which often leads to strokes or haemorrhages. He suffered a small stroke in May 1971, but in March 1973 he suffered a more serious one, and in June a triple haemorrhage behind his one remaining good eye left him to all intents and purposes blind. In *Les Mots*, in self-ironic mode, he had uncannily predicted the fate that would befall him: 'towards the end of my life, blinder even than Beethoven was deaf, I would grope towards the completion of my final work: the manuscript would be found amongst my papers and, disappointed, people would exclaim: "But it's illegible!".... Then, one day, out of love for me, some young scholars would attempt to decipher it: it would take them a lifetime to reconstitute what would turn out, naturally, to be my masterpiece.'[19] He was right in every respect save one: there would be no more masterpieces. The fourth volume of *L'Idiot de la famille* would remain forever unwritten.

The most disabling consequence of Sartre's blindness was that the activity that had defined his life – writing – was over, and so too, in a sense, was his life. Outwardly, he accepted this fact with a remarkable lack of self-pity, but in private it was a rather different story – a story chronicled in some detail by Beauvoir in *La Cérémonie des adieux*.

His reduced mobility and physical dependency on others (he subsequently developed diabetes) did not prevent him, however, from continuing to *act* to the best of his ability. But writing – his very *raison d'être* – was no longer possible: he could have learned to touch-type, but he could not have reread himself: rereading was a crucial stage of literary production for Sartre. In any case, typing would have been an unacceptable substitute: the physical process of writing by hand was somehow essential to his creativity. So there remained the voice. Indeed, everything Sartre 'wrote' after 1973 was in fact dictated or transcribed from tape-recordings. The year 1974 saw the publication of *On a raison de se révolter*, co-signed with Pierre Victor and Philippe Gavi, and which was an edited version of a series of *entretiens* (both 'interview' and 'conversation') between Sartre and the two young Maoists between 1972 and 1974. The motives behind that publication were pecuniary as much as intellectual: the money it brought in was used to launch, and keep afloat, the new left-wing daily *Libération*. Also in 1974, Sartre worked on the sequel to his autobiography in the form of extended interviews with Simone de Beauvoir, in the summer and autumn of that year; interviews that covered his literature, his philosophy and his personal life.

When considering the spoken work of Sartre's last years, it is perhaps as well to recall *precisely* what distinguished speaking from writing in his view. Notwithstanding his theorization of writing as communication in the 1940s (a view that many commentators erroneously assume to have been his final word), Sartre remarked on more than one occasion – especially in the 1970s – that the most important thing about writing, for him, was what he called 'style'. Style was what allowed the writer to hide, or to not-communicate, as well as to communicate. Bereft of style, the spoken word gave the speaker no place to hide . . . The most sustained, and contro-versial, practice of the *entretien* took place in the privacy of Sartre's flat, and occurred in the last five years of his life.

During the years of his involvement with the GP, he had formed a close relationship with one young Maoist in particular. Pierre Victor – whose real name was Benny Lévy – was a Jew who had been brought up in a Francophone family in Cairo. The family had left Egypt at the time of the Suez affair. Lévy (whom I shall henceforth call by his given name) had eventually landed at the ENS. After the dissolution of the GP in 1973, he and Sartre began to meet regularly to discuss the question that most concerned them both: the conditions of possibility of the establishment of a non-authoritarian socialism. Lévy would come to Sartre's flat every morning, and every morning the dialogue would recommence. Lévy also read aloud the books that Sartre himself could no longer read. Lévy was, at the time, officially stateless – which explains, at least in part, the pseudonym he adopted – but was later naturalized a French citizen thanks to Sartre's direct intervention with Giscard d'Estaing. Their relationship was also formalized in 1975, when Sartre made him his 'special secretary'. It is tempting to see their relationship as a belated attempt by Sartre to acquire a son to go with the (adopted) daughter he already had, but there are problems with this interpretation, not least that Sartre loathed the father–son relationship. To see the pair as master and disciple is also problematic: Sartre detested being cast as the master – even when he had been an actual master in his *lycée* teaching before the war, he had taught not by authority but by provocation and inspiration – and Lévy was no starry-eyed disciple: he had an astonishingly detailed knowledge of Sartre's work and was not afraid to critique and debate. He was, moreover, thoroughly conversant with theoretical Marxism – especially the work of Althusser. Sartre himself presented their relationship as one between equals: they addressed each other as 'tu' (something that scandalized Sartre's entourage). But this too is problematic: after all, Lévy was a nobody who had published virtually nothing and Sartre was the most celebrated intellectual in the world. Furthermore, Sartre was his employer.

Sartre's biographers have found it very hard to interpret this relationship, for at least two reasons. First, it was a private and isolated relationship, putting one strangely in mind of the way Sartre described another experience of being read to: 'All the while [my mother] was talking to me, we were alone and clandestine, far from men, from the gods and the priests, two does in the forest, with those other does, the Fairies.'[20] This kind of exclusivity was something that Sartre had always maintained. His personal life was compartmentalized to an extraordinary degree and always had been. Cohen-Solal claims that Michelle Vian and Arlette, for example, never really met until after Sartre died – despite their both having been his intimate companion for at least 25 years; similarly, Lévy and Arlette did not become friendly with each other until just three years before Sartre's death. His friends would come and go to the flat in Montparnasse, but effectively did little more than pass each other in the street outside. Second, the acrimony surrounding the last years of Sartre's life produced accounts of the period that bare the traces of that bitterness. Beauvoir's memoirs are still the most abundant source of biographical material on Sartre, but nobody would claim that they are objective; and *La Cérémonie des adieux* – covering the last ten years of Sartre's life – was the most 'partial' of all. It is a disturbing text, describing in painful, tedious detail the physical and mental decline of Sartre, but also insisting on the immense will to live that kept driving him to fight against the inevitable. On closing the book, one is unsure to what extent this was a widow's paean to the love of her life, and to what extent the bitter revenge of a woman against the man who, she felt, had ultimately betrayed her. In the end, it is perhaps both: a work shot through with the ambivalence that characterizes the 'work of mourning'. Her representation of Lévy is highly negative: she imputes self-serving motives to him, but is notably at a loss when it comes to understanding what Sartre himself got out of the relationship. Lévy, for his part, has said that Beauvoir had simply failed to grasp the nature of the roles that Sartre had come to ascribe to each of them: she was an unchanging past, but he was an open future.

Be that as it may, if Sartre's last years were marred by acrimony, suspicion and paranoia, the blame must lie ultimately with Sartre himself: to the end, in his personal life, he was the dramaturge who controlled the exits and entrances of his characters.

The simmering hostilities, fuelled by mutual incomprehension, came to a head in 1978. By this time, Lévy's own intellectual pre-occupations had taken a surprising turn: the atheist Jewish militant had discovered the Kabbala and the Talmud and, in the company of Arlette with whom he had become close since 1977, had set about their serious study. It was against this background that he organized a short trip to Israel in February 1978 for himself, Sartre and Arlette. The purpose of the visit was for Sartre to be able to discuss the Israel–Palestine conflict with a small group of Israeli and Palestinian intellectuals. The discussions were, by all accounts, superficial; but the storm really broke upon their return to Paris. Lévy had prepared a text arising out of the visit and sent it to Jean Daniel at the *Nouvel Observateur*. It was signed 'Sartre–Victor'. Crucially, Sartre had not even mentioned the text to the woman he called his 'little judge'.

Beauvoir, of course, found out about it, read it, and begged Sartre not to allow its publication: it was, she said, poorly written, feebly argued and under-researched. It would not have been the first time that Sartre published a piece suffering from all of the above defects, so the real problem lay elsewhere: for Beauvoir and the colleagues at *TM*, the piece did not truly represent what they took to be Sartre's thought. But Sartre had already given the go-ahead to Lévy and, for whatever reasons – cowardice, or defiance of the old guard perhaps – refused to go back on the decision. To compound matters, he also failed to inform Lévy of Beauvoir's opinion; Lévy found out from her directly, at a bad-tempered meeting of the editorial board of *TM* – the last he ever attended.

Conflicts and hostilities that had been muted now became open. And there was much worse to follow. The daily *entretiens* between Sartre and Lévy continued, and drifted more and more towards Lévy's preoccupation with Judaism. The intention was to collaborate on a joint publication of a radically new kind. Sartre spoke enthusiastically about the project – provisionally entitled *Pouvoir et liberté* – and claimed to see it as the culmination of a long reflection

Jean-Paul Sartre, André Glucksmann and Raymond Aron at the Elysée Palace, Paris, 26 June 1979.

on politics and ethics. In the same spirit, he proposed to Jean Daniel that the *Nouvel Observateur* should publish a long Sartre–Lévy interview in which he would summarize the work they had already done on the book and explain his new positions.

In February 1980 Sartre had let his 'little judge' read the text, but was bewildered by the violence of her response (tearful and furious, she reportedly flung the manuscript across the room and told him that he *could not* publish it). Her view, and that of the old-guard at *TM*, was that an old man no longer in complete possession of his critical faculties had been bamboozled by a forceful young man with an agenda of his own.

But Sartre was no longer listening to the woman who had been his lifelong literary and philosophical sounding-post, or censor. Lévy delivered the manuscript himself to the offices of the *Nouvel Observateur*. Besieged by phone calls from Beauvoir, Bost, Pouillon and Lanzmann, Daniel hesitated. At which point Sartre himself called him and – most unusually for him – used his authority to present an ultimatum: Daniel *must* publish the text, in its entirety, or he, Sartre, would simply take it elsewhere. The contentious text was published under the title 'L'Espoir maintenant' in three instalments: 10, 17 and 24 March. Today, the value and significance of the piece are still debated by specialists: did it really mark such a radical disavowal of Sartre's most fundamental concepts? The interviews turn around the possibility of an 'ethics of hope' and in fact cover many subjects: humanism, obligation and reciprocity, the future of the Left (or its lack of a future), fraternity and democracy. The 'dialogue' is not particularly elevated, but neither is it particularly contentious, until it turns to Judaism. Lévy brings Sartre round to this topic via a discussion of *Réflexions sur la question juive*, and it was doubtless this that so outraged Beauvoir and her friends: Sartre appears to be suggesting that ethics (as the ultimate goal of revolution) could only really be thought in terms of a certain *messianism*. This was the Sartre who had denounced any hope of salvation as an illusion or a confidence-trick; the Sartre who had described Existentialism as nothing more than the attempt to draw all the conclusions from a coherent atheism . . . It is doubtless significant that Beauvoir chose to end *La Cérémonie des adieux* with a posthumous reaffirmation of Sartre's atheism in an obvious attempt to dispel the whiff of messianism that hung over 'L'Espoir maintenant': 'my relations with other people are direct – he tells her – they no longer take a detour via the All-Powerful, I don't need God in order to love my neighbour.'[21]

Sartre only just lived to see the publication of 'L'Espoir maintenant'. On 20 March he was admitted as an emergency to Broussais hospital with a pulmonary œdema. Initially, there was no particular cause for concern, but then his kidneys stopped functioning and surgery was out of the question: he was too frail. From that moment, he was condemned. There were brief remissions, but his condition worsened and he lapsed into a coma from which he never awoke: at around 9 p.m. on 15 April 1980, he died.

6

The Death and Life of Sartre

The struggle to control the meaning of Sartre's life began within hours of his death. The struggle was waged both in and between the public and private domains.

A general public knew little or nothing of the troubled relations within the 'family' during the last few years of his life. Simone de Beauvoir was the first to break cover: *La Cérémonie des adieux* (1981) chronicled the physical and mental decline of Sartre throughout the 1970s. The inclusion of the interviews was clearly intended to imprint a 'final image' of 'what Sartre stood for' in the minds of his readers in France and throughout the world – even though the interviews had been conducted as early as 1974. Arlette El-Kaïm and Benny Lévy do not emerge with credit from the pages of Beauvoir's book. In December 1981 Arlette published an open letter to Beauvoir in *Libération*, warning her 'this time you have gone too far'.[1] Each woman used the ammunition she possessed. It was Arlette, not Beauvoir, whom Sartre had made his literary executor: she used this position to publish, in 1983, the *Carnets de la drôle de guerre* and the *Cahiers pour une morale*, with notes and an introduction. Beauvoir had control over other material, and published two volumes of Sartre's letters to her – and 'a few others' – in the same year. Benny Lévy broke his silence in 1984 with *Le Nom de l'homme: dialogue avec Sartre*.[2] The struggle over the image of the Sartre–Beauvoir couple did not end with Beauvoir's death in 1986: in 1990, her adoptive daughter, Sylvie Le Bon de Beauvoir,

Simone de Beauvoir and Sartre, Paris, 1980.

published Beauvoir's letters to Sartre, as well as her war diaries.
Cross-referring between Sartre's letters and war diaries and the
Beauvoir letters, one notices some curious lacunae in the latter –
suggesting that the editor was keen, even after the death of the
leading protagonists, to manage the *image* of the couple that they
had cultivated in their lifetimes.

The 'battle for Sartre' in the public domain began as soon as his
death was announced. Every national and local radio and television
station carried the news as a lead item; starting the next day, and
continuing for over a month, daily newspapers, weekly news magazines and supplements indulged in an unprecedented feeding frenzy.
The sheer volume of material was testament in itself to the magni-
tude of the figure who had disappeared. Not for the first time, the
Communists and the bourgeois right adopted strangely similar
positions. Both attempted to negate the significance of Sartre as a
political activist by abstracting him from history and praising the
timeless qualities of the Artist, the Writer or the embodiment of
the French Intellect. Articles and obituaries appeared on all five
continents. Commentators in Latin America, the Caribbean and

Africa were unanimous and sincere in mourning the 'loss of a friend'. In Brazil, the writer Jorge Amado considered Sartre to have been 'the most important man of the post-war period, the man who has exercised the greatest influence on the world today'. A discordant note was struck by a Palestinian journalist who suggested that Sartre's real sympathies had always been with Israel. *The Washington Post* opined that, even after 1956, Sartre had remained a Communist. *Iszvestia* devoted fully five lines to Sartre's passing.[3]

Once the shock had passed, the backlash was not long in coming. Each significant anniversary over the last 25 years has seen renewed coverage in newspapers and magazines. Since 1990 – as the neo-conservatives gloated in the wake of the disintegration of the Soviet bloc – the coverage has been particularly negative, particularly in France. News magazines such as *L'Express, Le Nouvel Observateur* and *Le Point* have repeatedly devoted their front covers to Sartre. Inside, readers have been called upon to 'forget Sartre', but the economic logic of these very publications prevents them from doing so: after all, his face and his name, even when dragged through the mud, still sell magazines.

The year 2005 – 25 years after Sartre's death and the centenary of his birth – was always going to be the most significant anniversary. It has been marked by dozens of international academic colloquia and scores of new books (commissioned for the occasion, or republished to coincide with it) as well as many reissues of old classics – often with significant 'revisions'.[4] His plays have been revived; the Bibliothèque Nationale has devoted its longest-running ever exhibition to 'Sartre the writer'; television and radio stations have broadcast profiles of the man and reassessments of his work.

But why? Writing in *Le Monde des Livres*, Michel Contat remarked in March 2005: 'Commemorations, commemorations! Magazines put Sartre on the front cover at the same time as wondering whether he should be burnt, or while stating that he no longer arouses anything but indifference – or occasionally both at the same time.' The testimonies, he continues, oscillate between denunciation and hagiography. But one can discern a qualitative difference between the testimonies of journalists and those of academic commentators. The latter have arrived at a stage of discriminating judgementalism – separating the wheat from the chaff. This is even true in the case of establishment intellectual historians such as Jean-François Sirinelli and Michel Winock – neither of whom could be accused of being left-wing firebrands.[5] Journalists, by and large, have contrived to give the public what they pretend to think they want: opinion (prejudice) and point of view (ignorance). In French publications, this is to be explained largely by the political coloration of the newspapers and magazines for which these journalists write. In Britain, the picture is interestingly different. It is only those 'serious' newspapers that fondly consider themselves to be centrist or 'left of centre' that have troubled to devote significant space to Sartre – presumably to cater for the presumed intellectuality of their readership. But in Britain the assessments of Sartre's life have been coloured less by the political positioning of the publication in question than by a characteristically British anti-intellectualism and gallophobia: in this centenary, also, of the *Entente cordiale*, national stereotyping and overt racism are apparently acceptable when directed at 'old friends'. A prime example, amongst many from the print and broadcast media, was to be found in the review section of *The Independent* of 17 June 2005. The two-page article purports to 'explore [Sartre's] legacy'. With an almost audible sigh of relief, the author concludes: 'despite the Sartre revival in the radical US,[6] it will probably be Sartre the artist-writer, rather than Sartre the political thinker, who survives'. An opinion one should certainly respect, especially when it is proffered by a scholar whose extensive knowledge of Sartre's work leads him to assert that *L'Idiot de la famille* was 'published only after Sartre's death'. The article ends engagingly: 'It is impossible to divide his work from the lingering, carefully crafted persona of the man: "the engaged [sic] intellectual" with rotting teeth, chain-smoking Gauloises in the Café de Flore'. Doubtless an image guaranteed to reassure all non-smoking British 'intellectuals' endowed with perfect dentition.

Of course it is possible to divide the work from the persona; it is also possible to seek to relate the work to the persona, but to do either it is first necessary to read the work. And this raises the question of who still reads Sartre. *Le Monde* conducted a series of interviews with thirty-something researchers in literature and philosophy departments in French universities. As arbitrary as the sample may have been, the results are borne out to a large extent by actual statistics relating to masters and doctoral theses completed in France. In French philosophy departments, Sartre is today – as he always has been – a marginal figure. Students of phenomenology read Husserl, Heidegger and Merleau-Ponty, but rarely Sartre. He has never been set as a subject for the *agrégation*. His literary theory no longer serves – if it ever did – as a theoretical model for students of *lettres modernes*. In postcolonial studies, the reference points are Foucault and Edward Saïd; Sartre's infamous preface to Fanon's *Les Damnés de la terre* is even perceived to have 'sunk' Fanon himself in the eyes of French readers (although he is currently undergoing something of a revival in the English-speaking world). In all of the domains Sartre occupied during his lifetime, he has been eclipsed as a theoretical reference point by more 'specialist' thinkers. As we saw in the last chapter, this trend had begun as early as the 1960s. All of this is due in part, no doubt, to the rigorous divisions in the French university system between philosophy and literature departments: Sartre, after all, melded those two activities to greater effect than any other twentieth-century writer – even Camus. But it is probably also due to the sheer *singularity* of his thought, and it is with the question of Sartre's singularity that we shall conclude.

The question of Sartre's continuing relevance or irrelevance – as indeed of the significance of his life – has for some years now been debated under the heading of his supposed 'mistakes': 'les erreurs de Sartre'. In France, as elsewhere, these 'errors' have been used to disqualify the whole of the Sartrean enterprise: a man who sympathized with the Stalinists, who worked with the Maoists, who justified 'terrorist murders' of 'civilians' in Algeria or Munich *must* have been wrong about everything. The illogicality of the argument requires no comment; but even those who concede that Sartre may have been 'wrong' about some things and 'right' about others are missing an important point. To understand this point, we have to return to what Sartre himself said about the vicissitudes of life after death.

The characters in *Huis Clos* are dead on earth – that is, they no longer 'realize a physical presence in the world'. This dramatic conceit was explicated at length in *L'Etre et le néant*. As long as I am alive, the meaning of my life is never fixed: it can always be modified by my choices and actions in the future, as well as by the actions and judgements of other people. A 'dead life' is one that can never again be modified from the inside (by the person who had lived it), but one whose meaning is henceforth constantly modified from the outside (by the living). The lives of the dead are taken up by the living: 'the characteristic of a dead life is that it is a life of which the Other makes himself a guardian.'[7] The living may adopt various attitudes towards the dead lives with which they are entrusted: they may choose preservation, oblivion or indifference. But even the billions of dead who have been forgotten individually do not cease to exist; they exist collectively: 'To be forgotten is, in fact, to be apprehended resolutely and forever as an element merged into a mass . . . it is to lose one's personal existence in order then to be constituted with others in a collective existence.'[8] The guardianship referred to here is a guardianship of meaning: the living henceforth decide on the meaning of the lives of the millions of dead – both the 'preserved' and the 'forgotten' – who silently haunt them; but not by deciding whether the actions of this dead

A scene from a production of Sartre's *Huis Clos* at the Théâtre de Potinière, Paris, 1946.

individual or that disappeared group *were* right or wrong – the process is far more subtle and open-ended: 'It is I and the men of my generation who decide on the meaning of the efforts and undertakings of the previous generation, either by taking up and continuing their social and political enterprises, or by making a decisive break and casting the dead back into inefficacy.'[9] As long as there are living men and women making the world and redefining humanity, the meaning of the lives of the dead will always be 'in suspense'. From this point of view, the question '*was* Sartre wrong?' can only be answered at the End of History (and then there will be nobody there to ask it or to answer it). It should be rephrased: 'will Sartre have been wrong?' The answer to that question lies not in Sartre's actions, but in our own. If, for example, we create a world in which social injustice is never questioned, in which misery is accepted as an accident of birth or in which torture is considered normal, then he will have been wrong – for as long as that world exists. And perhaps that is why the question is never asked in this way: from beyond the grave, Sartre reminds us of the responsibility of being human. This is why he remains an importunate corpse.[10]

References

Unless otherwise indicated, all translations from Sartre's work referenced in French are my own.

1 A Child in the Hall of Mirrors

1 Jean-Paul Sartre, *Les Mots* (Paris, 1964), p. 19.
2 Ibid., p. 17.
3 Ibid., p. 18.
4 Ibid., p. 61. See below, p. 122.
5 Jean-Paul Sartre, *Les Carnets de la drôle de guerre*, texte établi et annoté par Arlette Elkaïm-Sartre (Paris, 1983 and 1995), p. 506.
6 *Les Mots*, p. 97.
7 Ibid., p. 46.
8 Ibid., pp. 53–4.
9 Ibid., p. 130.
10 Ibid., p. 125.
11 Ibid., p. 161.
12 Ibid., p. 136.
13 Ibid., p. 193.
14 Ibid., p. 25.
15 Commander Aupick was the hated step-father of the poet Charles Baudelaire, whose mother, like Anne-Marie Sartre, had remarried after the loss of the child's father.
16 The early texts referred to in this section are all to be found in Jean-Paul Sartre, *Ecrits de Jeunesse*. Edition établie par Michel Contat et Michel Rybalka (Paris, 1990).

17 *Ecrits de Jeunesse*, p. 145.

18 See D. W. Winnicott, *Playing and Reality* (London, 1971).

19 *Les Carnets de la drôle de guerre*, p. 281.

20 Jean-Paul Sartre, *Lettres au Castor et à quelques autres* (2 vols), édition établie, présentée et annotée par Simone de Beauvoir (Paris, 1983), p. 10.

21 Ibid., p. 29.

22 Ibid., p. 30.

23 *Les Carnets de la drôle de guerre*, p. 538.

24 *Lettres au Castor* (i), pp. 45–6.

25 Simone de Beauvoir, *La Force de l'âge* (Paris, 1960), vol. i, p. 156.

26 Jean-Paul Sartre, 'Une idée fondamentale de la phénoménologie de Husserl: L'intentionnalité', in *Situations i* (Paris, 1947), p. 41.

27 Ibid., p. 40.

28 Jean-Paul Sartre, *La Nausée* (Paris, 1938), p. 15.

29 Ibid., p. 16.

30 Ibid., p. 11.

31 Ibid., p. 16.

32 Ibid., p. 24.

33 Ibid., p. 142.

34 Ibid., p. 141.

35 Ibid., p. 179.

36 Idem.

37 Ibid., p. 181.

38 Idem.

39 Ibid., p. 182.

40 Ibid., p. 185.

41 Simone de Beauvoir, *La Force des choses*, i (Paris, 1963), p. 58.

42 *La Nausée*, p. 39.

43 Ibid., p. 61.

44 Ibid., p. 246.

45 Ibid., p. 247.

46 Idem.

47 *Les Mots*, p. 211.

48 *La Nausée*, p. 142.

49 For a dossier de presse of *La Nausée*, see Jean-Paul Sartre, *Œuvres romanesques*, édition établie par Michel Contat et Michel Rybalka

(Paris, 1981), pp. 1701–11.

50 In *Œuvres romanesques*, p. 1807.

51 Ibid., p. 310.

52 *Œuvres romanesques*, p. 1807.

53 *Lettres au Castor* (I), p. 272.

54 *Œuvres romanesques*, p. 805.

2 Of Arms and a Man

1 Jean-Paul Sartre, *Situations* x (Paris, 1976), p. 175.

2 Jean-Paul Sartre, *Œuvres romanesques*, édition établie par Michel Contat et Michel Rybalka (Paris, 1981), p. 805.

3 For a discussion of these incidents and Sartre's reaction to them, see Andrew Leak, 'On Writing, Reflection and Authenticity in Sartre's *Carnets de la drôle de guerre*', *Modern Language Review* (1998), pp. 972–84, and 'Les enjeux de l'écriture dans *Les carnets de la drôle de guerre*: prolégomènes à une théorie de l'engagement', *Etudes Sartriennes*, VIII (2002), pp. 49–62.

4 *Les Carnets de la drôle de guerre*, p. 48.

5 Ibid., p. 55.

6 Ibid., p. 45.

7 Ibid., p. 55.

8 Ibid., p. 56.

9 Ibid., p. 614.

10 Jean-Paul Sartre, *Lettres au Castor et à quelques autres* (II), édition établie, présentée et annotée par Simone de Beauvoir (Paris, 1983), p. 147.

11 Michel Leiris, *L'Age d'homme* (Paris, 1939).

12 *Lettres au Castor* (II), p. 39.

13 Ibid., pp. 351–2.

14 Ibid., p. 538.

15 Ibid., p. 214.

16 Ibid., p. 538.

17 Cf. Jean-Paul Sartre, *Huis Clos* suivi de *Les Mouches* (Paris, 1947), p. 120.

18 *Lettres au Castor* (II), p. 82.

19 *Les Carnets de la drôle de guerre*, p. 538.

20 Ibid., p. 578.

21 Ibid., p. 580.

22 Ibid., p. 215.

23 Jean-Paul Sartre, *L'Imaginaire* (Paris, 1940), p. 372.

24 *Les Carnets de la drôle de guerre*, p. 538.

25 *Œuvres romanesques*, p. lvi.

26 'Forgers of Myths: the young playwrights of France', *Theatre Arts*, 30, no. 6 (June 1946). This article only every appeared in English translation; the quotation here is taken from *Les Ecrits de Sartre* (p. 374), where it is translated back into French by the editors!

27 Jean-Paul Sartre, *Pour un théâtre de situations* (Paris, 1973), p. 225.

28 *Les Carnets de la drôle de guerre*, p. 539.

29 Quoted in Annie Cohen-Solal, *Sartre, une vie 1905–1980* (Paris, 1985), p. 242.

30 Unpublished text quoted in Cohen-Solal, *Sartre, une vie 1905–1980*, p. 269.

3 The Price of Fame

1 See for example, Sartre's 'L'Ecrivain et sa langue' in *Situations* x (Paris, 1976), p. 41.

2 Simone de Beauvoir, *'La Cérémonie des adieux'* suivi de *'Entretiens avec Jean-Paul Sartre'* (Paris, 1981), pp. 389–90.

3 Michel Contat and Michel Rybalka (eds), *Les Ecrits de Sartre* (Paris, 1970), p. 123.

4 Jean-Paul Sartre, *Oeuvres romanesques*, édition établie par Michel Contat et Michel Rybalka (Paris, 1981), p. 729.

5 Jean-Paul Sartre, *Situations* ii (Paris, 1948), p. 16.

6 Ibid., p. 13.

7 Idem.

8 Ibid., p. 26.

9 *Combat*, 4 September 1944. Quoted in *Les Ecrits de Sartre*, p. 106.

10 Boris Vian, *L'Ecume des jours* (Paris, 1947).

11 Bernard-Henri Lévy, *Le Siècle de Sartre* (Paris, 2000), p. 49.

12 *Situations ii*, p. 43.

13 Jean-Paul Sartre, *Réflexions sur la question juive* (Paris, 1946), p. 110.

14 Jean-Paul Sartre, *Qu'est-ce que la littérature?* (Paris, 1948), p. 17.

15 Ibid., p. 55.

16 Ibid., p. 342.

17 Ibid., p. 350.

18 Jean-Paul Sartre, *Situations* III (Paris, 1949), p. 233.

19 Quoted in Annie Cohen-Solal, *Sartre, une vie 1905–1980* (Paris, 1985),
p. 406.

20 Jean-Paul Sartre, *Cahiers pour une morale* (Paris, 1983), p. 483.

4 The Shock of the Real

1 For an excellent history of *Les Temps modernes*, see Howard Davies,
Sartre and 'Les Temps Modernes' (Cambridge, 1987), from which these
statistics are taken.

2 Simone de Beauvoir, *La Force des choses*, I (Paris, 1963), p. 247.

3 Ibid., p. 208.

4 Idem.

5 Ibid., p. 275.

6 Roger Stéphane, *Portrait de l'aventurier* (Paris, 1965), p. 13.

7 Ibid., p. 12.

8 Ibid., p. 30.

9 Ibid., p. 31.

10 Ibid., p. 33.

11 *La Force des choses*, pp. 333–4.

12 Jean-Paul Sartre, *Le Diable et le bon Dieu* (Paris, 1951), pp. 251–2.

13 *La Force des choses*, p. 333.

14 Idem.

15 *Le Diable et le bon Dieu*, p. 57. English translates both 'salaud' and
'bâtard' as 'bastard', but we are dealing here with the *literal* bastard.

16 Jean-Paul Sartre, *Saint Genet, comédien et martyr* (Paris, 1952), p. 536.

17 Ibid., p. 81.

18 *Paris-Presse l'Intransigeant*, 7 June 1951.

19 *La Force des choses* I, p. 359.

20 Idem.

21 Jean-Paul Sartre, Philippe Gavi, Pierre Victor, *On a raison de se révolter*
(Paris, 1974), p. 33.

22 Most recently, Ronald Aronson in *Camus and Sartre: The Story of a
Friendship and the Quarrel that Ended It* (Chicago, 2004).

23 Camus had famously quipped that Sartre and his friends had never done more than point their armchairs in the direction of history.

24 Jean-Paul Sartre, *Situations* x (Paris, 1976), p. 220.

25 Jean-Paul Sartre, *Kean* (Paris, 1954), p. 79.

26 Interview in *Combat*, 7 June 1955.

27 *L'Express*, 9 November 1956.

28 Frantz Fanon, *Les damnés de la terre* (Paris, 2002), p. 31.

29 Jean-Paul Sartre, *Le Scénario Freud* (Paris, 1984), p. 570.

30 Jean-Paul Sartre, *Les Mots* (Paris, 1964), p. 19.

5 No More the Universal Intellectual

1 Jean-Paul Sartre, *Critique de la raison dialectique* (Paris, 1960), p. 44.

2 Ibid., p. 236.

3 'L'homme est-il mort?', *Arts et Loisirs* 38, 15 June 1966, p. 8.

4 See Michel Sicard, *Essais sur Sartre* (Paris, 1989), p. 368.

5 Flann O'Brien, *At-Swim-Two-Birds* (London, 1939), p. 9.

6 Jean-Paul Sartre, *Cahiers pour une morale* (Paris, 1983), p. 380.

7 Jean-Paul Sartre, *Les Mots*, (Paris, 1964), p. 208.

8 Ibid., p. 61.

9 Simone de Beauvoir, *La Cérémonie des adieux* (Paris, 1981), p. 275.

10 See *Les Mots*, p. 205.

11 *Essais sur Sartre*, p. 369.

12 *Les Mots*, pp. 199–200.

13 Quoted in Michel Contat and Michel Rybalka (eds), *Les Ecrits de Sartre* (Paris, 1970), p. 455.

14 Ibid., p. 442.

15 Quoted in Cohen-Solal, *Sartre, une vie 1905–1980*, p. 605.

16 Jean-Paul Sartre, *L'Idiot de la famille*, 3 vols (Paris, 1971; 1972), p. 653.

17 *Les Mots*, p. 20.

18 Idem.

19 Ibid., p. 173.

20 Ibid., p. 41.

21 *La Cérémonie des adieux*, p. 558.

6 The Death and Life of Sartre

1 *Libération*, 3 December 1981.

2 Benny Lévy died in 2003, but his publisher, Verdier, has cashed-in on the Sartre centenary by republishing the work referred to here, as well as two other Lévy texts: *L'Espoir maintenant* and *La Cérémonie de la naissance*.

3 This section is indebted to Annie Cohen-Solal, *Sartre, une vie 1905–1980* (Paris, 1985), pp. 658–62, as well as to the author's own dusty and badly referenced scrapbook.

4 The re-issue of François George's excellent *Deux Essais sur Sartre* (Paris, 1976) is a case in point; the author – now calling himself François George Maugarlone – explains: 'I've cut out a few Lacanian phalluses and added a little Aronian water to my Marxist wine'.

5 Jean-François Sirinelli, 'Sartre–Aron, les frères ennemis', *Le Monde des Livres*, 11 March 2005, p. vi; Michel Winock, 'La passion de l'erreur . . . et de la justice', *Le Nouvel Observateur*, 3–9 March 2005, p. 62.

6 Hardly a revival: Sartrean theory has been 'applied' in the USA to subjects such as sexism, homophobia, anti-black racism etc. for at least the last fifteen years.

7 *L'Etre et le néant*, p. 599.

8 Ibid., p. 600.

9 Ibid., p. 601.

10 'Bref, ce mort insupporte encore beaucoup'. Michel Contat in *Le Monde des Livres*, 11 March 2005, p. i.

Bibliography

Works by Sartre

L'Imagination (Paris, 1936)

La Transcendance de l'ego (Paris, 1965 [1937])

La Nausée (Paris, 1938)

Le Mur (Paris, 1939)

Esquisse d'une théorie des émotions (Paris, 1939)

L'Imaginaire (Paris, 1940)

L'Etre et le néant (Paris, 1943)

Les Mouches (Paris, 1943)

Huis Clos (Paris, 1944)

L'Age de raison (Paris, 1945)

Le Sursis (Paris, 1945)

L'Existentialisme est un humanisme (Paris, 1946)

Réflexions sur la question juive (Paris, 1946)

Morts sans sépulture (Paris, 1946)

La Putain respectueuse (Paris, 1946)

Baudelaire (Paris, 1947)

Situations I [Essais critiques] (Paris, 1947)

Les Mains sales (Paris, 1948)

Situations II ['Qu'est-ce que la littérature?'] (Paris, 1948)

La Mort dans l'âme (Paris, 1949)

Situations III [Lendemains de guerre] (Paris, 1949)

Le Diable et le bon Dieu (Paris, 1951)

Saint Genet, comédien et martyr (Paris, 1952)

Kean (Paris, 1954)

Nekrassov (Paris, 1955)

Les Séquestrés d'Altona (Paris, 1959)

Critique de la raison dialectique, vol. I: *théorie des ensembles pratiques* (Paris, 1960)

Les Mots (Paris, 1964)

Situations IV [Portraits] (Paris, 1964)

Situations V [Colonialisme et néocolonialisme] (Paris, 1964)

Situations VI [Problèmes du marxisme, 1] (Paris, 1964)

Situations VII [Problèmes du marxisme, 2] (Paris, 1965)

L'Idiot de la famille. Gustave Flaubert de 1821 à 1857 (Paris, I and II: 1971; III: 1972)

Situations VIII [Autour de 68] (Paris, 1972)

Situations IX [Mélanges] (Paris, 1972)

Un Théâtre de situations (Paris, 1974)

On a raison de se révolter with Ph. Gavi and P. Victor (Paris, 1974)

Situations X [Politique et autobiographie] (Paris, 1976)

Oeuvres romanesques (Paris, 1981)

Lettres au Castor et à quelques autres (Paris, 1983)

Cahiers pour une morale (Paris, 1983)

Le Scénario Freud (Paris, 1984)

Critique de la raison dialectique, vol. II: *l'intelligibilité de l'histoire* (Paris, 1985)

Mallarmé. La lucidité et sa face d'ombre (Paris, 1986)

Ecrits de jeunesse (Paris, 1990)

L'Espoir maintenant (Paris, 1991)

Les Carnets de la drôle de guerre [nouvelle édition augmentée d'un carnet inédit] (Paris, 1995 [1983])

Théâtre complet (Paris, 2005)

Works by Sartre in English translation

The Imaginaire, trans. Jonathan Webber (London, 2003)

The Transcendence of the Ego: A Sketch for a Phenomenological Description, trans. Andrew Brown (London, 2004)

Nausea, trans. Robert Baldick (London, 1963)

Intimacy, and other stories, trans. Lloyd Alexander (London, 1949)

The Emotions: Outline of a Theory, trans. Bernard Frechtman (New York, 1948)

Being and Nothingness: an Essay in Phenomenological Ontology, trans. Hazel E. Barnes (London and New York, 1958)

The Flies, trans. Stuart Gilbert (London, 1946)

No Exit, trans. Stuart Gilbert (New York, 1967)

The Age of Reason, trans. Eric Sutton (London, 1947)

The Reprieve, trans. Eric Sutton (London, 2001)

Iron in the Soul, trans. Gerard Hopkins (London, 1950)

Existentialism and Humanism, trans. Philip Mairet (London, 1980)

Anti-Semite and Jew, trans. George J. Becker (New York, 1995)

Three Plays: Crime Passionel [sic], *Men without Shadows, The Respectful
    Prostitute* (London, 1969)

What is Literature?, trans. Bernard Frechtman (London, 1993)

Lucifer and the Lord: A Play in Eleven Scenes, trans. Kitty Black (London, 1952)

Saint Genet: Actor and Martyr, trans. Bernard Frechtman (London, 1988)

Kean, or, Disorder and Genius, trans. Kitty Black (London, 1954)

Nekrassov: A Farce in Eight Scenes, trans. Sylvia and George Leeson (London,
    1956)

Loser Wins: A Play in Five Acts, trans. Sylvia and George Leeson (London, 1960)

Critique of Dialectical Reason, vol. I, *Theory of Practical Ensembles*, trans. Alan
    Sheridan-Smith (London, 1976)

Critique of Dialectical Reason, vol. II, *The Intelligibility of History*, trans.
    Quintin Hoare (London, 1991) [unfinished]

The Words, trans. Bernard Frechtman (New York, 1964)

Between Existentialism and Marxism, trans. John Mathews (London, 1974)

The Family Idiot: Gustave Flaubert 1821–1857, trans. Carol Cosman, 5 vols
    (Chicago, 1981–93)

Sartre on Theater (New York, 1976)

*Quiet Moments in a War: The Letters of Jean-Paul Sartre to Simone de Beauvoir,
    1940–1963*, trans. Lee Fahnestock and Norman MacAfee (New York, 1993)

Notebooks for an Ethics, trans. David Pellauer (Chicago, 1992)

The Freud Scenario, trans. Quintin Hoare (London, 1985)

Mallarmé, or, the Poet of Nothingness, trans. Ernest Sturm (University Park,
    PN, 1988)

Hope, Now: The 1989 Interviews, trans. Adrian van den Hoven (Chicago, 1996)

War Diaries: Notebooks from a Phoney War, November 1939–March 1940, trans.
    Quintin Hoare (London, 1984)

On Sartre

The present study has drawn heavily on the seminal biography of Sartre by Annie Cohen-Solal, but the other biographical studies listed below (Bertholet, Hayman, Lévy) all have their own strengths. The biotextual study by Wickers is one of the most perceptive books on Sartre in recent years.

Barnes, Hazel E., *Sartre and Flaubert* (Chicago, 1981)

Bertholet, Denis, *Sartre* (Paris, 2000)

Catalano, Joseph, *A Commentary on Jean-Paul Sartre's 'Being and Nothingness'* (Chicago, 1980)

———, *A Commentary on Jean-Paul Sartre's 'Critique of Dialectical Reason'*, vol. 1 (Chicago, 1986)

Caws, Peter, *Sartre* (Boston, MA, 1979)

Cohen-Solal, Annie, *Sartre 1905–1980* (Paris, 1985)

Contat, Michel et al., *Pourquoi et comment Sartre a écrit 'Les Mots'* (Paris, 1996)

Contat, Michel and Michel Rybalka, *Les Ecrits de Sartre* (Paris, 1970)

Drake, David, *Sartre* (London, 2005)

Goldthorpe, Rhiannon, *Sartre: Literature and Theory* (Cambridge, 1984)

Hayman, Ronald, *Writing Against: A Biography of Sartre* (London, 1986)

Howells, Christina, *Sartre: The Necessity of Freedom* (Cambridge, 1988)

Idt, Geneviève, *Les Mots: une autocritique en 'bel écrit'* (Paris, 2001)

Jeanson, Francis, *Sartre par lui-même* (Paris, 1955)

Lévy, Bernard-Henri, *Le Siècle de Sartre* (Paris, 2000)

Louette, Jean-François, *Jean-Paul Sartre* (Paris, 1993)

McBride, William, *Sartre's Political Theory* (Bloomington, IN, 1991)

Wickers, Olivier, *Trois Aventures extraordinaires de Jean-Paul Sartre* (Paris, 2000)

Review

The principal forum for scholarly debate on Sartre and Existentialism in the English-speaking world is *Sartre Studies International* (published by Berghahn Books Ltd: www.berghahnbooks.com).

Internet

There are literally thousands of sites devoted to Sartre – of highly variable quality. The following sites are reliable and authoritative and provide links to other useful sites.

http://www.jpsartre.org
http://www.alalettre.com/sartre-intro.htm
http://condor.stcloudstate.edu/~phil/nass/home.html
http://www.sartre.org
http://fr.wikipedia.org/wiki/Jean-Paul_Sartre
http://plato.stanford.edu/entries/sartre

Photo Acknowledgements

The author and publishers wish to express their thanks to the following sources of illustrative material and/or permission to reproduce it.

Photo Bibliothéque Nationale de France: p. 121; photo courtesy of Editions Bonnier Archives, Stockholm: p. 19; photo Library of Congress, Washington, DC: p. 67 (Office of War Information Photograph Collection, Washington Division, LC-USW3- 057448-C; photo J. Sherrel Lakey); photos Rex Features: pp. 6 (© Lipnitski/Roger-Viollet, 4430550), 56 (© Rex Features/Sipa Press, 229116B), 117 (© Rex Features/Sipa Press, 515620A), 131 (© Rex Features/Sipa Press, 23626A), 141 (© Rex Features/Sipa Press, 515610B); photos Roger-Viollet (courtesy of Rex Features): pp. 66 (© LAPI/Roger-Viollet, LAPI-134-29420), 106 (© Lipnitzki/Roger-Viollet, LIP-012-053-081), 107 (© Collection Roger-Viollet, RV-807763), 111 (© Lipnitzki/Roger-Viollet, LIP-138057-039), 145 (© J. Cuinières/Roger-Viollet, JAC-11619-16), 150 (© Lipnitzki/Roger-Viollet, LIP-134-025-001).